MICHAEL'S THOUGHTS

BY

MICHAEL KELLEY

International Standard Book Number 0-87012-885-X
Library of Congress Control Number 2018900755
Printed in the United States of America

McClain Printing Company
Parsons, WV
www.mcclainprinting.com
2018

The struggle can be relentless in the transition from the state of awake to that of asleep. Awake seems to become more active within the mind at this juncture than any other time. She found herself here quite often but eventually asleep does win out and takes ownership of the stage. Asleep she finds herself within a dream. In her dream, she is running. Her eyes are closed tightly as she runs. Anxiety consumes her as she is unable to see what she is running from. She has to rely on what she hears and feels along the way to find some clarity of where she is. They seem to be chronologically depicting events she has experienced in her life. She can hear the laughter of children and then sounds of a wedding. Then it changes to the sounds of the tide coming in and out and she can feel the warmth of the colors orange and red. It gets cold and her running becomes difficult through what feels like snow high upon her feet. The cold then gives way and she becomes consumed in the sound and the smell of a summer rain. Even with the moments combining one after the other she still carries that fear of what she may be running from. She tries to open her eyes but cannot seem to gather the courage to do so. Finally, with one great burst of effort and desire to see she opens her eyes in one desperate flash. Immediately she sees the sun teasing through her bedroom window. The colors, seeming to burst through the curtain and the shapes are stealing entry at every open possibility. The sound of birds singing seems to be directed at her by the volume and the melody. Awake has once again taken control as the dream fades quickly. The minds eyes remained just long enough within the dream to see. It is with this vision that a sense of contentment and happiness fills her. In her dream, she was not running away but toward the endless possibilities the lay before her. The events depicted within her dream were the moments that will be with her always. Don't let fear distract you from the enjoyment of the show.

The water of the pond was a deep green in color but ran clear through your fingers. It was his turn on the rope swing. He backed up to get the best advantage he could and then ran with all his might until his feet left the ground. Out over the pond he waited as long as he could wait and not begin to swing back. He let go of the rope and found himself weightless as he waited to enter the water. The moment he hit the water everything went dark. The moon was shining just enough for him to see he was in his bedroom. He sat up in bed and reached to turn on a light. He was in his room but somehow it just felt different. Had he dreamed of being with his friends at the pond having fun? Morning came and he went to the bathroom and as he looked into the mirror only to be horrified by what he saw. The person he saw was not him or at least did not look like him. Quickly he ran to the kitchen to see his mother cooking breakfast. She turned and said “good morning honey”. Confused he asked her if he looked alright and she replied handsome as always. The day continued to be a one of discovery as he found himself different and everything else the same. In time, he came to accept it without understanding. It was like he was a totally different person thrown into an unchanged world. He went on to graduate high school, get married and raise a family, and grew old. His life happened just as it was supposed to but he always felt deep within that it was not the life the person before the rope swing would have lived. He tried to talk about it when he was younger but no one believed or understood so he just learned to hide it away. The day came when his time was done in this human existence. The final sound of this life was the squeal of the machine he was hooked up to. The sound of the machine went silent and all went dark. SUDDENLY he found himself submerged in water and fighting to find the surface. As he reached the surface he felt the sun on his face and so bright that he could not see clearly. He swam to the edge of the water and was greeted by others as he arrived. Confused and weary from the plunge and swim he found himself looking to understand. He could still hear the scream of the machine and he wondered how this could be. As he sat there he put his head into his hands and as he slowly opened his eyes. In the reflection in the water was the person he was long ago. He looked up and around in amazement and then silently laughed to himself. "What a dream". Or was it?

The room was shadowed and the chill bites to the bone. The faces were all unknown and distant. My position in the center of the room enhanced the vulnerability I already felt within. I watched the man stand and stare in his direction. He would then turn toward the crowd and speak and then turn immediately toward me. He and the crowd we all focused on me. The silence was profound as they all waited for me to answer to the words he spoke to the crowd. My heart was coming thru my chest as I summoned the courage to respond. The exact words he spoke evaded me but I did manage to "I don't have the words but my feelings are real". This time his voice was deep and hinted of sarcasm as he looked into my eyes and said "what you feel is irrelevant and you did not answer the question. Shall I repeat it for you?" I said yes to buy some time but his question was now clearly planted in my mind. Again, he turned toward the crowd and spoke the question to them that I was expected to answer. I was diligently searching for the answer. As they all sat there staring at me with judging eyes I wondered to myself. "Is the answer something they want to hear or is it something I know but cannot see?" he spoke my name with apprehension as the crowd remained silent but listening. In this silence came the sound of the door opening to the room but no one was there. As the door slowly glided to an open position a light entered the dark room and focused its illumination upon me. As I struggled to see until my eyes adjusted the answer came to me so clearly. With a confident and excited voice, I spoke my answer "I am". "I am responsible for my sadness as well as my happiness". He and the crowd looked defeated with my answer. As he sat back down another voice said "case set free".

She stood by helpless as her heart and mind argued over what was best. She listens to her heart say that sometimes what is best won't seem right. With that thought she began to walk and quickly started to run. She ran as fast as she could and ran all the way to the end of the peer. As she leaned over the rail to see she saw that her ship had sailed. She waved but knew that no one was looking. She watched as it went out of sight. When it could no longer be seen she began to cry. Leaning over the rail she could see his reflection in the water. She watched and cried as her tears slowly fell onto his reflection. The more she cried the more his reflection became unrecognizable as her tears tore through it. When she could no longer see him in the water she stood back from the rail. She wiped the tears from her face and walked home by the light of the moon and stars. As she looked toward the stars she saw one star so much brighter than the others. Upon that star, she prayed for forgiveness and promised to appreciate the gifts she was given should she ever be blessed again. That night sleep was very short and after many attempts she gave up and rose early in the day. At the beauty of the dawn she decided to go for a walk. The beach was beautiful as the early morning sun cast its orange spell. As she walked she could hear voices in the distance. As she came closer to the voices she could see many as they pulled their small boats ashore. She didn't know what was happening and they paid no attention to her as she passed. Then faintly she thought she heard her name. She turned to look but only saw all those who were still making their way to shore. Again, she heard her name but this time she could see someone running toward her. It was him but she continued to just stare in disbelief. It was really him. The excitement grew within her almost to burst just as he met her and embraced her so tightly they became one. No words were spoken for seemed the longest time until she said "what happened, you were gone". He looked at her as he still held her limp body in his arms. He said "the weather was clear but not long after we were underway a great rain came upon us and the sun shined at the same time. It rained so much that we could not bail it fast enough and had to abandon ship and return home. It was a strange rain in that every drop that I would taste while trying to save myself tasted like you. I saw you at the peer but you could not hear me. I thought, I mean, you were there?" She said nothing. She just pulled him close enough so again they were one just as the sun freed itself from the sea and glowed through them forever.

Lost, alone, and hidden became his existence. One day led to many without the sun. The false sense of security became more pronounced with each passing day. As he looked to the sky the weather was frightful in all directions. Forward was the only direction that showed even a glimmer of hope but appeared just behind the darkest cloud. It would require a leap of faith to expect that once through the storm the light would shine again. Once he convinced himself that there was nothing to lose, into the storm in front of him he journeyed. The storm was violent and damaging but once through the skies opened up with a glorious invitation. The sun warming his face he found courage, previously unknown to him. The sense of security he once thought he needed from outside he now found easily from within. As he joined others around him he noticed their strangeness. He had come from a dark and desperate place and all he brought were the moments and memories collected. Those around him were caught up in the search for things they could not carry with them. He resisted the desire of this world for him to join them and walked his own path. In his leap of faith, he learned that he had everything he would ever need. Guided by that faith the voices of others soon became silent and his journey became one of comfort and contentment. He came to discover that his entire human existence was merely the day before the first day of forever. He did not look back but he did wonder if all would understand this would it change what they believed they would be able to take with them. What will you choose the day before the first day of forever?

Traveling can be sometimes tiring and frustrating. A turn can quickly guide you a direction you had not intended to go. It can bring you to a place you never imagined being. I can tell you of one such experience and leave it for you to ponder. The day started out clear and bright but as I traveled I would come upon dark clouds that would bring down the sky upon me. A wrong turn led me to an opportunity for rest and I stopped in hopes of regaining the clarity of my purpose and destination. As I became lost in my thoughts trying to see where I went wrong I noticed a small little shop beside me. I seemed a tiny building and the sign above the door read TIMES DESIRES. On the door was another sign that said ALWAYS OPEN LIMITED TIME. As I opened the door I heard the sound of another door shutting. As I stepped in I found myself within a long hallway. It was so long that I couldn't see the other end other than a faint glow. Along the walls on both sides, top to bottom were just pictures. Each picture was not marked with a price but with a number of hours or days. It didn't make sense to me until much later. There were pictures of everything you could imagine. As I walked and looked at the pictures down the seemingly endless hallway I began to understand that each picture was listed with the amount of time it might take to possess them. There were lots of pictures of children laughing and many more of families clearly depicted to show the love. There were couples embraced and even pictures of the sun, moon, and stars. There were many images of things like houses, cars, boats, and numerous other possessions like that. You could see awards, titles, and money as well. As I finally came to the end of the hall and could the glow be coming from on the other side of the window in this door. This door was much smaller than the one was to enter the shop. There was no possible way to get through this door if you wanted to carry anything out. There was another hand-written sign just above this door that read DID YOU SPEND WISELY? As I open the small door I heard the sound again of another door closing. As I made my way through this door and turned to pull it shut I found myself standing again at the front door. Somewhat confused but yet somewhat enlightened I left to continue my journey. DO YOU SPEND WISELY?

The park had been closed for many years. It was such a sight to see and experience in its day. The stories drove it to extinction. The stories were of ghost that would haunt the house of mirrors. People said she would appear in the mirrors as soon as someone would enter. The moment you would look at her she would begin to scream “please don’t look at me! Get out!” Soon no one would go to the park out of fear. Years passed by and the park fell into ruin. No explanation or understanding was ever found. Superstition prevented anything else from interest in the property so it just sat there sad and misunderstood. One night a storm would engulf the area in darkness and danger. A traveler caught in the storm was desperately seeking shelter. He happened upon the park but was unfamiliar with stories. As he walked through the park he came across the house of mirrors and sought shelter within. He just stood inside the door for the longest time just watching the storm outside. The storm did finally calm and all became quiet. Feeling safe at this point he decided to stay the night and set out again in the morning. He began to look around and search for good place to sleep the rest of the night. The mirrors were dark and dusty and some were even broken from time passing. He lighted a candle from his pocket to light his way. With this light, he noticed something out of the corner of his eye and quickly turned to see a very beautiful older woman about his age standing before him. As he looked into her eyes she just stood there silent and still. He asked "who are you"? Still looking into her eyes, he saw tears begin to roll down her cheek. She then spoke in a soft and warm voice. "Is that what I look like?" Their eyes so locked upon on another that neither could notice anything else about the other. He was confused at first but soon realized the answer to her question. Without looking away he reached to wipe a tear from her cheek and said "yes". Your soul is who you are and it can only be seen through the windows of the eyes of another. The candle finally gave way to a sunrise beyond imagination. No more stories were ever heard about the ghost in the mirror.

Worn and battered by the battle of life a couple makes it home. They both encountered the storm but each made it safely. Soon after arriving the storm would take the power and left them in the cold and dark night. They settled into one room and shared a blanket to keep warm. They had one candle burning alone in the darkness and silence. The sound of the candle was very pronounced and it would flicker with such rhythm and shadow that it became hypnotic. Soon they were sound asleep and without the normal noise needed to drown out the silence. They would awaken much later but found themselves still surrounded by candle light and silence. She spoke first to tell that she had dreamed such a strange dream. She told of her dream where she was in the forest. It must have been fall because the colors of the leaves painted everything. It was warm and the only sound I could hear was the wind blowing through the trees and the sound of your heartbeat as you were with me. You were protecting me in such a way that I have never felt that free. He gazed at her through the shadows of the candle. He told of a dream he had had and it was exactly like hers except in his dream she was there protecting him. They both laughed at the oddity of this experience. Suddenly the candle began to flicker violently as it struggled to stay alive but lost the battle as the room went dark. A moment after the room went dark the power came to life once again. It took a moment for their eyes to adjust to the brightness and clarity. Once adjusted she fell again into his arms and held tightly. He pulled her even closer as they become one. He gently leaned and kissed her on the head and brushed the amber and orange leaves from her hair.

Strong in the belief that al he was came from within and not a mirror's perception he traveled along his journey hidden from that which did not serve him. Birthday's mingled with life's rite of passage moments accumulated to fill the shelves of the library of his growth. Even the survival of long lapses of inactivity of individuality did not diminish the vision he held clearly in his mind. Then one day he would, even with the knowledge of knowing better, look into that rear-view mirror. His perception would be forever changed. He knew it was not a true image but that did not diminish the magnitude of it. All the years he successfully avoided the demon did nothing but give it more strength to impact at this delayed confrontation in his journey. With this event, he realized that he should have confronted and came to terms many miles ago. He knew this too he would overcome but it was like ruining a perfect recipe on the final step and would require much more repeated effort to achieve the designed vision. Even with the pain and torment that came with this delayed experience he was now able to fill that empty space in his library of growth. In the end, the fear that causes you to avoid and hide does not possess the power you perceive that it does. Avoidance does nothing but delays the inevitable and steals the most precious gift we are given with time.

Against the power of normality, I wonder. Why as blessed beings we have the unique ability to pass thru life as though all that exists is what we know. It's amazing what a drive down a back road that you have never traveled before and witness history blended with present and occupied by life that is not in our realm of known. I wonder as I pass by what their life is about, are they subjected to the same obstacles and joys that we think only exists in our own existence. The truth is that each of us is but a tiny piece of a much larger picture and story. We strive for more but we haven't even learned how to use what we have yet. Our imagination and vision is much more powerful than we allow. Until we learn that we are designed to grow as a population and not as individuals we will never reach our potential as beings and see greater things than we dare imagine. Compassion, love and kindness yield unmeasurable results of progress. I challenge us all to imagine outside our walls and reach out and spread the love for life and all things that exist within it and beyond it. We must realize the box exists in order to see outside of it. Happy travels.

The storm was one in which the damage seen was miniscule once compared to that unseen. He stepped out from the shelter that would soon show betrayal. Each discovery of damage led yet to another he was unaware of. Fight he would but struggle he will in the journey between dark and light armed only with truths painted black or white. Forward is better than back, right is the opposite of wrong, and good wins out over bad. He found the world after the storm to be crowded and noisy. So much so he felt lost within it having to concentrate so much to not be trampled and silenced. He soon realized that moving forward did not mean following the crowd but choosing his own path. Once on his path the crowd dispersed and the noise turned into quiet bliss. In this sanctuary of his spirit he discovered the he was never lost but merely hiding. Hiding from the black or white choices we all must make in the discovery of our journey. Black or white is only the title to the book of life's truths. Dark and light are just shades of the same color. Good always wins out over bad but requires patience, trust, and faith. Someone with which to share his journey had always been a desire. He, like many others, would look forward for such a soul and when nothing could be seen he would look back with guilt and desperation. Once again, he found the answers do not come from the title but from the many chapters that make up the book. Some will spend their entire journey and not realize that God walks with us, not ahead or behind us. So, in our search for souls to share our journey we should look for those who walk with us and beside us. The width of life is just as endless as its length. From the storm, he found the vision to see the colors hidden between black and white.

As she watched she could see the little girl ever so slowly coming down the steps of the small white house. The porch seemed to go all the way around. The girl was wearing I simple white dress and her hair in bows. She was heading toward other children waiting for her on their way to school. Her mother was standing at the door waving and saying "I love you". Her sister, a few years younger, looked on from a window above the porch. Then she saw both little girls going to school. The mother was again standing at the front door. The warmth coming from the open door she could feel on her face as she watched. She could hear the laughter from the within the house as she watched. Mother, Father and the girls would leave together from time to time heading out on sort of adventure. She watched as young men would arrive to see the girls, young women now. Friends and family were always coming and going and joy was consuming as she watched. A wedding in the back yard was beautiful though it brought joy and sadness as she watched. Grandchildren now drew even greater joy and sadness as they would leave to return another time. These times she saw the mother and father standing at the bottom of the steps waving and saying "we love you". As she watched the house became empty and silent over time. A voice distracted her from watching and as she looked away from the mirror in the small white house. She turned to the real estate agent and said we will take it. What you leave behind is just as important as what you take with you.

As the sun went into hiding it was a day of one season. As the sun rose it awakened all to a day of another season. The thick blanket of snow gave a sense of purity. It also came with a sense of confinement to most. A little girl who was staying with her grandparents saw it only as a reason to spend more time being the center of attention. Her mother was set to pick her up but with the weather would be delayed. As her grandmother was busy fixing breakfast, Martha was sitting in her grandfather's lap as he sat in favorite chair next to the warming fire of the fireplace. Upon the fireplace mantle she saw a picture of her sister who had passed and immediately she became sad and began to cry. What's wrong, why do you cry. She pointed to the picture and through tears asked "why did she leave". Her grandfather hugged her tight as only a grandfather can. She did not leave; she went to help others and to be with your daddy. She will always be with us. She is not only with us she is in everything. All you have to do is to think of her and you will see and hear her. You know that sound your grandma makes when she shakes out the rugs? Yes, she sniffled and replied. If you think of them and listen very carefully you will hear that sound. It is the sound makes as angels use their wings. With a look of astonishment but total belief she wiped the tears from her eyes. No matter where, no matter when she will always be here for you until the time comes when god needs you. And when that time comes you will join her in helping others like she does. The thought he planted in her mind brought a smile to her precious face. She hugged him as only a granddaughter can and said I love you. Softly from the kitchen grandma announced that breakfast was ready. Martha scampered off to the kitchen leaving grandpa to follow. He rose from his favorite chair slowly. As he raised his head the strangest breeze blew at his face and continued through him. Bewildered by the breeze he paused in silence. Suddenly the overwhelming sound of a rug being shaken filled the room. Stunned he looked around the room to see nothing. Reflecting for only a moment he then smiled ever so compassionately. He knew!

Awakened from a short sleep by what sounded to be a sudden fall of rain. He rose to look to the window but the night was clear and dry. I was strangely quiet and still he found as the squeaky window fell open. Closer he looked through the space with no screen to obscure his view. Still nothing could be seen and all was silent beyond deafness. The smell of charcoal lay heavy in the air. With dismissal, he sat at his desk with his thoughts. Again, the sound of the sudden rain or perhaps it was the wind. Again, he jumped to the still open window but all was silent and still. Again, he returned to the desk but confused and lost in contemplation of understanding. This had been a rough year but he made great progress in standing up once again after falling. He had laid down this night with a great headache from the conflicts of the day. Those days that he felt powerless to change and truly follow his heart. He began to feel sick to his stomach and it grew like a fire through his chest and settled in his head. So loud and strong that he could hear the beat outside of his body. Again, the sound rushed around him. This time the sound was the same but it sounded more like the heavy bags of clothes he would toss around as he went to do laundry. This time he could feel the sound stop in his head. He did have a headache so he thought he might just be sensitive. This time he lay back down but wide awake with his thoughts. There was battle continuing within his mind. He had learned a great deal over the last year and felt what was once motivating to him was now a conflict with every step and every directive. This time no sound but the pain was sharp and lasting in his head. He felt like there was a fight inside his head but that didn't make sense. He decided to take something for the headache. He went to the medicine cabinet. The door he had left open earlier. He took the medicine and held his head down to the cold of the sink to his forehead. He stood and just the medicine cabinet door. He looked into the mirror on the cabinet door in the dimness of the night light. Forever he would be changed by what he saw. Not one image but two distinct images of himself did he see. Both images were screaming at him "CHOOSE". He ran back to the supposed security of his room. He shut and locked the door. He went to the window and pulled it shut and locked. He drew the blind and the room was dark with the exception of the alarm clock as it blinked 12:00 over and over. He slowly turned toward his closet and opened the door and brought to view in the dim light a mirror. He looked toward the mirror with his eyes shut so tightly that it was making his head pound back and forth making the sound that had awakened him earlier. With a burst of courage, he sprung his eyes wide open. Fear engulfed his entire body as he waited for his eyes to adjust to the light. When clarity returned he saw the image of only him. Just one image and no voices could be heard. With relief, he leaned toward the mirror and caught himself with his hand. His hand landed on something unfamiliar. As he jumped back he saw a sign that he had posted on the door earlier that year. The sign read "life is about choices you make not choices you contemplate".

Awakened from what seemed a deep sleep I found myself at the bottom of a great canyon. The river was roaring like a constant thunder. The sides of the canyon were jagged and steep. Turning away from the thunder of the river I could hear the sounds of birds singing like they were in a state of contentment and happiness. Nature itself was green and growing and full of life beyond my understanding of the meaning of life. Even with all the serenity surrounding me I felt I needed to go beyond the walls of the canyon in search of something I could not even explain let alone understand. I searched the walls for the opportunity for escape. Many times, I tried and failed and other times I would reach a restful landing but only to find no advancement possible from there. So, I would make my way back down and search for another route. All this time of searching and trying the river became silent and birds were not singing and nature looked to be standing still. From my many attempts, I was scratched and scarred and now went with great apprehension and fear. My search that was once carefree was now clouded by doubt and fear, but continue on I must. The longer and harder I tried I found the reason for the journey was less about me and more about expectations of me. With this insight, I just accepted the situation as what was meant to be. Once again, the river roared, the birds sang, and nature spiritually surrounded me. I found the strength to cherish the happiness within me despite the assumed expectations that had once haunted my thoughts. As contentment surrounded me I heard what sounded like a voice. It was faint and I could not hear it clearly. What do you want? I said. Again, the voice came, louder but still not clear to me. What? I yelled. This time the voice came back as a yell and was clear and direct. MICHAEL!! Get out of that creek and come eat supper right now! Quickly I did find my path.

Be it darkness or light, your path is free to choose. In the light, your path is guided by vision and hope but in the darkness your path is guided by pain and fear. We choose to avoid that which is painful and in the darkness, we stand still. To truly move forward one must travel in the light or forever still in the darkness you shall remain.

Go forth with caution but let it not lead your heart. Come forth with the wisdom that sets you apart.

Step forth to those who come later in your heart. Bring forth that passion you possessed in the start.

Go forth with release of life's chains on your heart. Come forth with as much in the end as was in your start. Step forth stronger to those who may deserve your heart. Bring forth no regret of loss continued on your part.

Death is a very harsh reality and tragedy. Its affect is to those who remain. I don't believe the death of our human bodies is the end but just the beginning. I believe we evolve from the human state to that of a spiritual one like a butterfly evolves from a caterpillar. I believe this existence is created by god just for that purpose. I do not believe god is responsible in this life to the point of controlling all things we may call bad or good. I believe he is a source of guidance and rescue along this journey. Time is not relative to him so our existence is merely a blink. Things happen every day and everywhere to good people by my definition as well as bad.

I believe that death is only the beginning by the way someone who has passed has the ability to be in our minds forever. I also believe we are quick to blame god when something happens close to us that is bad but we neglect to show appreciation when good things happen. I also believe that when something bad happens to someone, they have the hope and assurance of crossing over to a place where there is no pain or suffering. Again, I repeat that I don't think anything bad or good is of god's construction or design. His only hope is that we learn from everything as we aspire to be the spiritual beings that he had envisioned. Yes, I believe god also is a dreamer of dreams and a wisher of wishes. The underlying message in all interpretations of religion is that he will always be here for us and the promise of a better life once evolved.

Chase, it I must with desire like lust. Chase, it I can with freedom of man. Chase, it I will as it appears to stand still. Into the wind I push forward for ownership. The closer I feel yet its pace unchanging. Forward still I go on this magical Journey. Time passes by and it seems to mock me as it taunts me with its magical colors and shadows. It appears to hide but I still can see. Then it goes dark and I think, is it tricking me. Focused I remain to where last I saw. Forward I go, to the point of awe. Then suddenly I see, but not in front of me, but again mocking from behind. I stop my pursuit as I see the truth. It is I that has been caught. I should feel sad but I feel encouraged by the journey. the journey comes with a lesson so true. Go forward you must but take heed of behind you. Until another day sun!

Thoughts attack me with the opinion that all things that happen or do not happen in life happen in such a way as to demand a reaction from us. Reaction is a thing we are taught and led to believe that it should be avoided. Philosophers say be happy with what you have and better things will come. Motivators say dare to dream and what you think about will come to you. I propose a different theory from a nobody point of view. Nothing will last forever whatever forever may be. For some it may be a moment and others may see it as a long span of years as perceived by man. God created life and I can't imagine a clock or calendar came in to play with creation. I also propose that life was meant to be a journey not a destination or a situation without hope. I propose we continually grow and evolve and not fear change but embrace it as part of life and thus find contentment within conflict. But what would I know.

Alone and surrounded by darkness we find ourselves. Into a mirror we gaze and beg the answer to the question, who am I. As bits and pieces of the answer start populating our thoughts we hesitate with resistance to the concept of being defined. We wish not to be limited by definition but to be anything and all things as god intended. We then become consumed with banishing the fear of not falling into the expectations of society. Most spend their lives following the rules and being happy based on what is expected to be happiness. Few choose to live their lives open to the endless possibilities and infinite definitions of life. I choose the path of enlightenment not the road of entitlement. May you also be blessed by the awakening of the soul and spirit in the realization that spiritual happiness come from inspiration not definition.

Drawn by the light a man accepted it as the end of his human life. Once he arrived at the source of the light he found himself standing in the middle of an open meadow. Its edges lay beyond his ability to see. A voice he heard and assumed was speaking to him because no one else was in sight. The voice asked "how would you describe your human life?" after a little thought he responded. "I was a very hard worker and achieved many goals; I experienced many happy moments and many sad ones; I was loyal, caring, and committed". The voice then said "I did see you spend the majority of your life working to achieve the goals and wishes of a few". "Were these few responsible for the gift of your life and did they offer you the truths and guidance that I offered you?" this time without thought he answered "no". Can you see or hear any of those few here where you stand? "No" he replied. Did you have such a lack of trust in me that you chose to pursue those things that you independently could attain or experience? Did those things bring you the joy and fulfillment that I offer you? The man, unable to answer the question, stood silent with his head down in shame or regret. Softly the voice said "I forgive you and assure you that I will always have faith in you. If you have faith in me I will always guide you. If you trust in me I will give you courage. If you live your life seeking to achieve those goals I hold dear your life will be blessed. Those few will no longer decide how you will define the human life given to you freely". The man looked up from the ground. He was no longer standing alone in a meadow he was standing once again within his human existence. Momentarily bewildered he looked up from his desk and was forever changed but yet true to the creation.

Is it not a shame when your greatest fear is from a system created to protect you? A system clouded by the pursuit of making all things either black or white. Designed to serve the people but ultimately serving those in financial or political control. How many people have to suffer at its hands before we take back our freedom and stand up for what is right and just based on gods design not mans.

Happiness can be generally defined as the ability to control your own thoughts and mind. Thinking happy thoughts will somewhat magically bring happiness upon you and around you. I pose a somewhat different perspective. I don't believe our thoughts and mind were ever meant to be controlled. We hang on to negative thoughts or events demanding answers or direction. Not every moment requires a reason. We spend so much energy looking for the reason or explanation that we miss the opportunity to learn and grow from it. We will spend moments, years, or even lives in search of something that was already there. This life we are given was meant to be lived not controlled or directed. We are not the directors of life. Whether we have a long or short life, it is in preparedness for the next. All things that happen, happy or sad, are experiences we need in order to evolve into what we shall become. The truth in understanding comes from the realization that answers or understanding serve no purpose. What is important is to feel and grow from all experiences. Faith is the answer to all things and in faith we find the ability to let go and move forward. The conflict we create by trying to control our thoughts and mind do more harm than good. I believe less control and more freedom of expression with faith as the anchor would be our true destiny. We are shown answers and understanding but we refuse to see them. When we refuse to see our own answers, we create a conflict of control upon something that was never meant to be controlled at all. Be who you are, do what you enjoy, show love, be kind, show support, laugh and cry, just live. Let go of the definition of life man has created and remember who created it. Have faith in where you are going and live the journey.

Happiness shown when between destinations but sadness is hidden in regret of lost time.

The void created by the absence of decisions and thoughts of choices expressed in mime.

The many possible outcomes of the choices you imagine only create more hidden sadness.

But the hour glass of time we turn again to create that temporary state of happiness.

Successful escape is possible by choosing a beginning rather than predicting an ending.

Choose a beginning that makes you happy and enjoy the journey of your soul mending.

Life is not living out a book already written it's about having faith and creating one unwritten.

In the very beginning an emotion or feeling was needed to bring the recognition to all things positive. Happiness was created and was instructed to go out in the world touch any and all things. Happiness was excited for the opportunity to share itself with the world and went out with the greatest optimism and hope. Happiness spread throughout the valleys, the rivers and the mountains supreme. It worked so hard and spread itself from the soil below to the stars above. The colors, smells, shapes and textures all were touched by happiness. Things were good but over time happiness felt overwhelmed by a foe whose objective is to undo any and all goodness. This new foe was sadness. Sadness became an obstacle to happiness and it was not understood why sadness was created and allowed to spread to everything or anything happiness had touched. In frustration and sadness happiness asked why, why would this be allowed? Why would you create my opposite and allow it to destroy me? The answers to the pleas of happiness finally came. Happiness, I did not create sadness. Sadness comes from within you. Without knowing sadness, one cannot truly know happiness. When you become sad the message you send is that of sadness. When you feel overwhelmed by sadness also remember that happiness is within you and it is up to you to find the happiness within you and again you will spread happiness over the land.

It was a long and winding road. It wasn't even really a road as it showed traces of gravel but was mostly dirt. The middle and sides were grown up with natures flowers. Traces of what used to a fence line were only visible by the random forgotten fence posts now entwined with green. The wind blew slightly but only evident as the tree tops gently swayed. No sounds of civilization, depending on your perspective, were able to be seen or heard. It was that perfect kind of silence but it was filled with the sounds of life. A man lost but found within his own mind, walked the journey alone. The man was aged and wise from life. He felt so comfortable and at home along his journey. So confident in the silence the was singing an old song that touched his heart and allowed the expression he was feeling. The man's song was light in tone but as his journey continued to no particular destination it became more pronounced. His words and rhyme not exactly giving the impression of being completely accurate to the writer intention but the passion he shared made up for the mistakes and failures. Hey, if you happen to see the most beautiful girl in the world. Tell her I need her. Tell her I miss her and tell her I love her. He also smiled and laughed at himself as he walked and sang and reflected with hope and faith going forward alone. The message he sends is to find that place and person within ourselves and sing our own song for all the world to hear and have faith that good things come to those willing and ready to accept them.

For a moment imagine that which expressed as theory may truly be possible. Imagine a soul so ashamed or perhaps unaware of itself that it begins and continues life betraying its own true self. A soul that has generous ability to love and care for another soul. Unknowingly so afraid of rejection that it dares not risk the truth. Imagine this soul desperately needs companionship to feel whole. Imagine this soul finding other souls in which to enter into the concept of companionship early in life and consistent through life. Years or lifetimes go by without even a hint of the dark secret coming to light as it is even lost to the soul itself. One day after much reflection and much analyzing a theory comes to light. The soul out of fear now understands that it does not project itself but to the contrary adapts itself and becomes that which the companion soul seeks and desires and hides all things related to the real attributes and qualities of the soul. The beginnings are good but time becomes the worst enemy as the hidden soul fights from within to be seen and heard and finds success in incrementally larger proportions as time goes on until eventually the soul becomes not that which it originally presented itself to be. No harm is or has ever been meant but the hidden souls desire to be loved for being itself grows until the point of separation. Regret and remorse for time lost and true soul mate delayed grow stronger as well over time until finally the courage of the hidden soul is fierce and the leap of faith becomes easily attained and freedom is as inspiring as the setting sun or more in common with the rising moon. Unfortunate is what the journey could be labeled but necessary is the true answer. There are no answers or explanations of this soul's journey but the message to be learned is always just be yourself and trust god to handle everything else if one were to imagine for a moment

In my life I have come to fear this demon more than any other. Without even my own awareness I maintain my guard vigilantly. He has been the better of on more than one occasion. It is from these encounters I draw the fear and guarded soul that walk with me always. Some would say my fear is misguided but challenge their thoughts with my experience. Upon occasion I catch him sneaking up on me. Even with a quick response I only manage to see the tail of a flash faded red from the shadows in which it hides. My understanding is lost in why he may attack me but not anyone else I may see or think of. Its damage is going so much deeper than body or flesh. He focuses the attack on my heart and soul. I have recovered from the attacks but never will I be the same. I blame him for the guarded wall I constantly maintain with apprehension of another attack. It is not my wish for anyone else to fall victim to his vengeance but it would make more sense to attack another before me. Maybe it is in my strength that makes me an ideal victim and outlet for his demonic desires. One day I vow to catch and conquer this demon but until then I just say "damn you cupid".

In the beginning they were there. I never noticed the struggle that must have been. One could accept that as a compliment to be worth that amount of effort. They didn't just suddenly leave. It started with short absences and gradually grew longer and more often. Then one day it became clear that they were gone. It was just something I would have to accept. They never offered any explanation or understanding. The difference; was not something I could ever get used to, or appreciate. I then found myself leaving more often and for longer intervals. Confrontation offered me the choice to change but I could or would not. I couldn't imagine being something else to be there for something I didn't want. I could have asked them to change but I believe everyone should be themselves. I would always know it wasn't them. Both being gone but yet not is complicated. Each being less and less who they are and regret builds exponentially. Time passes quickly as you live in a state of shadow and numbness. Then one day you realize that they were never there and everything they are now mocks you and takes advantage of you. You decide to leave for good so you can be yourself and not waste any more time as an audience member watching your own life. The conflict rages now. Taking back the ribbon, they won for their performance because it becomes clear they cheated and misrepresented their intentions and qualifications. In society actors make a good living. But in the end the scale they receive for their performance pales in comparison to that they lost or never had in the first place.

In the beginning we ride looking into the wind so kind
With little thought or concern for past or that left behind
That for which we seek or search fails to even cross our mind
It is just a race and to all other things we find ourselves blind
You won't need to know what it is you want for
Until you want to know what it is you need for
The next part of the walk we spend looking behind
Stumbling and falling forward but differently blind
This time it will be regret that is taking over our mind
As we look for that we may have missed or left behind
You won't need to know what it is you want for
Until you want to know what it is you need for
Another part we spend standing still yet busy of mind
Wondering if ourselves that which we seek to find
But with no success the concept leaves our mind
Then suddenly without searching the miracles we find
You won't need to know what it is you want for
Until you want to know what it is you need for

It is just the place I go every day. Some days are dark and grey and others are colorful and bright. Each time I visit it is different but at the same time very familiar. At first, I watch and observe but quickly I become involved and engaged in the activity and the surroundings. There is some sort of energy there that inspires and seduces me. What started as a curious choice has evolved into a motivating addiction. Sometimes it is quiet and serene like a warm blue ocean tide under the moonlight and then other times I find it loud and intense like a jet taking off just above my hands. Like any addiction I suppose I don't see it as so but I just see it as a need to be whole. Sometimes I interact with people I know and sometimes it is people I don't know yet. I do realize that the more I go there that it becomes more difficult to leave and believe that is where I belong and that is where things are real as opposed to where I come from. It does however provide clarity and understanding to where from I come. I can remember visiting some time ago but I can't remember why I stopped. Today I found myself standing at that edge of the blue ocean tide. The moon was full and bright and the air was warm and soothing. I left there with again the feeling that all things are plausible and possible. My vision clearly enhanced as I am able to see things that are important and relative to a good life in the place I come from. Anxiously I await my next visit to that place called my imagination and soul.

It stood tall in the middle of a public park. It was in full bloom and glory. The contrast of the green of its leaves and the golden yellow of the apples it bore as its fruit seemed in perfect harmony with nature. Some of the apples already fallen to the ground like gifts for the taking. Others hang from the branches awaiting their time. The joy and blessings the tree offered shown abundant by all that passed by. Some would gather from the ground and others would find pleasure and fulfillment from the ones just within reach of picking. A man sitting alone on a bench nearby fell witness to all the events in front of him. With a sense of jealousy, he rose from his bench and walked toward the tree. Probably the largest apple and most likely the most rewarding from his perspective hung high and out of reach. The temptation of that apple was so great he decided that he would climb that tree to achieve the prize. Branch to branch he climbed. Branches were breaking under his weight, and other apples falling to the ground below him. He continued on without regard for the harm he was doing and focused only on the achievement that would set him apart from all the others. Finally, he was within reach of the prize. As he reached for the golden apple the branch below him broke and sent him violently to the ground. As he lay on the ground looking up he could see the apple he hoped to attain. Suddenly it released its grip from the branch and was falling toward the man. He reached up to catch it but saw it grasped by another hand before he could touch it. The hand belonged to a woman. She was wearing a long and flowing white dress. Her hair was long and flowing. Behind her a light shined brightly bringing definition to what looked to be wings. He looked into her eyes and was overcome by her beauty. She did not speak but he could hear the words she spoke to him. "Young man, I pray you have learned the lesson of your actions but your body did not survive the fall". As she gently tossed the apple to him the light behind her consumed him and he knew.

It was a night like no other. The sky was filled with dark clouds but they were moving with intent as the moon outlined their shape. The anticipation was similar to that of an opening curtain to a play. As they separated and the moonlight grew stronger and broader a stranger appeared from the edge of the clearing. He sat tall and proud in the saddle but made no attempt to draw attention to himself as he rode into the clearing and toward the openness that lay in front of him. His armor was dull and worn. It was said that he had spent many a year committed to a cause but was now free. The world he came back to was as much a stranger to him as he was to it. He settled in with the impression of making a new life for himself. He kept to himself and rarely talked to anyone. Those that came close enough to see him said he looked to be older and his face showed the signs of wisdom and experience. His eyes so deep and blue that they offered the perception that so much more lay within. He remained in his quiet solitude and only came to town for supplies once a week. The woman who ran the store was the only person he seemed to take any interest in. an accident had left her without the ability to speak but he seemed to communicate with her fondly. He would bring her things he had created from his heart more and more often. Being that he would not enter the store unless alone no one really knew any true details. But they did say that always as she left her smile would throw shadow at the sun. His face never changed and was always without emotion. His life previously must have left its mark on him this way. There came a day when strangers arrived to town. They were harsh and brutal toward others and brought great fear upon the town. They were doing and taking anything, they wanted. The town was in hiding but was no defense as the pushed their way from place to place. They did happen upon the store the knight would visit weekly. He was due later that day. The strangers were vandalizing the store but soon turned their attentions to the woman who ran the store. Fearful for the woman, a child did run to the home of the knight and told him but the knight did not respond. The strangers were ignorant to the woman not being able to speak and took it as a rebellious spirit. A spirit they had no taste for. Suddenly at the edge of town the knight appeared. He was wearing his dull and worn armor and was heading toward the store. He entered the store without hesitation and the door closed behind. No one was close enough to see but the sound of struggle was ominous. It became silent for what seemed an eternity. The door opened and out came the knight with the woman by hand. The rest of the strangers had gathered outside the shop. The knight sent the woman off to safety as he turned toward the strangers. He looked at the strangers and immediately began walking toward them. Some of the town's people had come from hiding. Motivated by his courage they joined him one by one as he continued toward the strangers. The strangers watched as the group grew larger. Hesitant to confront the knight they did turn and run. As they left town the knight stood alone in the street be the town's people behind him. He turned to face the town but just stood there silent. The woman from the store came from where she was hiding and the town's people parted to give her clear passage. There she stood in the street face to face with the knight in the street with the town looking on. She appeared hurt and bled the color of her lips. She pulled both her hands to her heart and then threw them toward him. He stood silently with no response. She stepped close enough to touch him. She wiped the blood from her chest and laid her hand on the worn armored chest of the knight. She then drew what looked to be the outline of a heart on his chest. She then put her hands to her heart then laid them on the one she had drawn on his. Momentarily silent and still he did turn and walk toward where his horse was tied. The town and the woman were confused by his behavior. Again, he sat tall and proud upon his horse. He rode toward the end of town away from everyone still watching. Suddenly he turned and rode with thunder toward the crowd and the woman. Stopping just beside her he offered his hand to the woman who drew his heart. He pulled her on the horse in front of him. He then spoke "my name is Valentine". They rode away together in silence.

It was a quiet, colorful, lazy fall day. A youth alone with his thoughts is exploring and wandering the countryside. Each step screams of the fallen leaves in the otherwise silent surroundings. The wind just blowing enough to let you know it is there but leaving everything undisturbed. Through the trees grown up as to hide the vision of a house, He sneaks quietly as he can to get a closer look. The look of the house tells of being empty and forgotten for some time. Mustering the courage, he peers through window so concealed by time that he had to brush away a spot in order to look within. Suddenly frightened he jumped back by the sights from within. Regaining his composure, he again looked through the window. It didn't make sense what he was seeing. There was a family within sitting at a dinner table. It appeared to be Christmas by the way the decorations glimmered and a Christmas tree glowed with happiness and joy. The sounds were muffled by the window but he could hear what sounded to be joy and laughter. Again, with confusion he wondered how this could be that the outside lost and forgotten but within was so full of life. The longer he watched the more compelling it became for him to go inside. It was like it was calling to him so familiar but not. No longer could he stand watching so he went to where the old and aged door stood. He knocked once ever so slightly and waited but nothing. Again, he knocked with the purpose of awareness and in doing so the door slowly opened about half way creaking the entire distance. He said hello but no response. Hello again he said with volume but no answer. He pushed the door the rest of the way open again creaking the distance. He was confused as he walked in to see nothing but an old and forgotten house looking within just as it had looked from the outside. He wandered around finding nothing of the vision from the window. He walked past an old dirty mirror and something made him find it strange. Back he stepped to the mirror and the vision he saw was of an old man. Long he looked until he realized the old man was him. He laughed as he left the house and went on his way and his words upon leaving echoed within the house. Life is about the moments you cherish and take with you forever.

It was early February from where he came. Snow and bitter cold seemed to be the permanent condition. Confining and depressing to most living here. A time of hibernation and awaiting the warmth and renew of spring. One man's faith had grown weak in the belief that spring or renew would ever come. The test of his journey was particularly rough on him over the last couple years. From somewhere out of the blue the weather opened a window with a taste of spring. The man inspired by the day made a choice to escape even if only for a few days. The feel and taste of the ocean warmed by the sun is where he decided he would go. The time it took to get there was somehow lost from his memory. All he knew was that he had arrived as he walked out under the sun painted beach. The sun on his face felt warm and healing. He looked to the sun, and then to the sea. He noticed a large blue kite sailing high in the wind just down the beech from where he stood. It was very early and the beech seemed to be empty. Being curious, he walked to where the kite seemed to be from. He could see the string but not where it was grounded or by whom. As he walked around the beach he saw that the kite was anchored in the sand and no one was around. He stood there and looked around but no one to be found. Then he heard what sounded like children laughing. He looked toward the sound and two kids were heading his way. It was a little boy and girl. They were each carrying a bag of something. He stepped back as they approached where the kite was anchored. Hello mister they said as best they could, being out of breath from the run. He also said hello and asked them if it was their kite. The kids said yes. They said "we wrote a thank you note to god and we have to get it high so he can read it". That is a very nice thing to do kids. You did get it pretty high before you gave up though. They said "we didn't give up; we went to get more string".

It was in a time long lost and forgotten. A captain of a large and majestic ship would dock in search of provisions and additional crew to continue his journey. He entered a tavern seeking food and drink. Upon entering he saw another man attacking what seemed to be a mere boy. The stranger was a very large and threatening man. The captain sternly asked the stranger to leave the boy alone. The stranger said mind your business. The boy steals from me. What did he steal? The stranger replies food from my plate. The captain looks on for a moment then replies to the stranger. You look far from starving and the boy looks in need of a meal. Leave the boy alone. The stranger, overcome by anger, moved toward the captain but the captain did not move. The captain, despite being smaller than the stranger, just stood his ground with confidence and his facial expression did not change or relinquish any ground. The stranger looked away from the captain and stepped away. I was finished; I have no time for these trivialities. As the stranger left, the captain looked at the boy who couldn't have more than twelve summers. Go ahead and eat boy, you look as though you need it. The boy rose from the ground where he lay and said thank you sir. Boy; you do not need to thank me for doing the right thing. He then made his plea for additional crew to hire. If you are up to it, we set sail at dawn. I captain the ship named HTIAF. Someone spoke up and said what language is the name of your ship. The captain just kept walking out of the tavern as though he had not heard the question. At dawn the captain stood surprised as the boy stood first in the line to hire aboard. Where is your family boy? The boy placed his hand to his heart. The only family I have are within me sir. The captain stood silent until he stepped to the side and allowed the boy aboard. Many days had passed since the boy joined this captain and crews journey. On one such day it grew dark and the sun nor the moon were visible. The captain gave orders to prepare for a storm. A storm he suspected was soon to confront them. The wind had taken on a violent attitude and the sea resembled more a mountain range. The wind and the waves grew stronger and larger as the crew watched from below secured. The captain stood alone at the wheel as he steered a path through the storm. A crewmate beckoned of the captain. Shall we make it through captain? The captain, without changing his focus, did reply. Only with gods will shall we find our way. The waves grew so tall that as the mighty ship came over the top of each wave, the sensation of weightless was overwhelming. On one such wave the captain lost his footing and fell. Hitting his head, he became unawake and lay there at the mercy of the storm. The crews below were not aware of their captain's fate. The boy, also below, was watching the entire time and told the crew. He asked for them to help the captain but their hesitation was unwelcomed. The boy came from below and found the captain and secured him to ship. He then went to the wheel and took control of the ship. The crew wonder how he would be able to steer the might ship without the experience or strength. They as much as gave up and began preparing themselves for their demise. Long through the night the boy steered and stood his ground. Many hours later the captain would awake to see what looked to be the boy steering the ship. He yelled for his crew for help. The crew also stood questioning how it was possible. The boy's clothes were the same but something looked different. It was just past dawn and the sun was just emerging from the ocean ahead. The captain again yelled but this time it was for the boy. BOY, is that you. How did you do this? No answer came from the boy. Again, the captain yelled. BOY, what is your name. This time the boy responded. My name is Will. Only will, asked the captain. The boy tied off the wheel. He then slowly turned toward the captain. The boy was no longer a boy. He was a man strong and tall. His long hair flowing in the breeze and his eyes shined the most brilliant color of blue. He smiled and seemed to restrain a laugh as he said, I am GOD'S WILL. Captain and crew were stunned and confused by the answer. Will then turned back to the wheel. He raised his arms high and looked up as if to be summoning the heavens. At this exact moment the sun freed itself from below the brilliant blue ocean with such brightness that it blinded the captain and crew. When the captain and crew regained their ability to see, will was nowhere to be seen. He had vanished. All aboard came forward in search but not to find him. They then looked to the blue water as his escape. Long they also searched the water but will was not to be found. The ocean water was blue like they had never seen. The water also was so still that it looked as though they were adrift within a blue mirror. Suddenly, a crewmate exclaimed look! The name of the ship was painted clearly but as the blue water reflected the name it clearly read, FAITH.

It was usually a long ride. Passing the time looking through the window and imagining all the other worlds as you pass by them or the signs of what were or what will be. It was one of those family reunion functions or something similar. It was usually in the summer and everything was green and it was warm and smelled of honeysuckle. The wind was gently whispering the sound of the sun pulling the water from nearby lake toward the heavens. Most the boys my age were satisfied to contemplate the pride in their possessions that they carried in their pocket but there are is always one like myself who was more interested in contemplating life in search of the why's and how's. Those thoughts are interrupted as you arrive and that sudden sense of awkwardness comes over you. The mect and greet game starts and it is tense but eases with each and every hello. The awkwardness fades away as you find and settle in with familiarity. On one such adventure of this nature at this point I gained the courage to separate myself from the group and was enjoying the day with my own thoughts. Sitting there on this big rock with what felt like green carpet all over it I looked beyond my environment with no expectation but with curiosity. At the far end of what seemed to be a road that ran parallel to some railroad tracks. The tracks and the road as well seemed to be forgotten in time as the grass and weeds were grown up in and around them. The rain from the prior day had filled many a puddle and I expect the sun was working its magic on them just like the lake. A long way off I saw what looked to be a girl alone. She was wearing a ball cap with her hair in a long pony tail, T-shirt and jeans. I wonder what she carried in her pockets I laughed to myself. She was kicking what looked like a pop can but I couldn't tell for sure. She continued up the road toward me. She would kick the can forward sometimes and other times she rescued it from the tracks or water holes back to the center of the road where again she was able to make greater strides. It appeared to be sad as she was alone but so was I. Finally, she came close enough to where I was that I could hear and see her clearly. She looked my way and waved and said hi boy. I was a little startled but I did compose myself to return the hello. I again spoke and asked her if she was alright. She responded with I'm great, why? I have watched you struggle with that can all the way up that road as if something were bothering you and you were lost in your thoughts. She looked at me bewildered and the turned and looked toward where she had come. After a pause she turned back to me and said heck no boy, look how far I have come!

It was Valentines and Daniel was waiting for his flight to board. He was headed to a meeting for work. Once on the plane he found himself sitting next to an older man. The old man asked "are you headed to see your sweetheart". No, I am traveling for work. I don't have a sweetheart. The old man said "well, that's a shame". They talked the entire flight about anything and everything. The old man's wife had passed but he was bringing her flowers for valentines. He talked about many things but they always came back to her. Daniel asked how he knew she was the one. She answered the question correctly son. He went on to explain what the question was and the answer he sought. Many years have passed since Daniel's brief encounter with the old man but the story of the question would always be with him. He had been in and out of relationships prior to this encounter. Daniel was a creature of habit so every day off work he managed to get he would sit on the peer of a local lake. The silence was calming and encouraging. Season to season he sat there in the silence and the spender of nature. Even in the winter it had a unique offering. He would sit and look into the water as anyone would pass by. If a woman would sit close by and ask him what he was looking at, he would ask "what do you see?" the answers were many and varied from nothing to myself to just water. All of which were not the answer he was hoping for. After time he lost faith in ever getting the correct answer as the old man had described. Still out of habit he would still ask any woman who might sit close the question but he didn't expect anything. On one such occasion a woman sat close. He had seen her walking by many times but she had never sat on the peer. As usual she would ask Daniel what he was looking at. Daniel in return would ask "what do you see". She took a little longer than most in giving her answer. While Daniel waited he imagined her saying fish or the sky. She gently touched him on the shoulder with what seemed to be excitement. She looked at the water and then back to Daniel and said "I see us". Daniel was not prepared or expecting that answer. He leaned toward her and gently touched her on the arm with excitement and said "correct".

The journey of life is not meant to be easy or straight. There is no right or wrong road. there is no road at all. Life is a spiritual journey filled with signs and suggestions. But it requires faith so, the mind can imagine and see the signs. It's when we lack faith that we invent reasons for things that happen in our lives. It's when we regain faith that the signs achieve clarity once again. It takes the loss of faith to appreciate faith renewed. We are all merely children sent to discover enlightenment each in our own way. Stay true to your heart and trust your faith and you will open your imagination to the reality that all things are possible and all things are for a reason. Stop looking for why and look forward to what's next.

The day was clear and bright but just enough so to bring sadness and sorrow to those without a plan to engage it. A man of some age found himself gifted by the day as well as the sorrow. After much thought he decided a ride through the country might bring him closer to living than he believed his life to be. This day he found the courage to choose away the road he knew and to follow a road less traveled. The sound of his bike provided a rhythm conducive to the organization of his thoughts and spurred new ones and clarity seldom experienced. The road he was traveling was unfamiliar and his pace was not a concern. Everything ahead of him lay open and opportunistic and everything behind him was visible only through the mirrors like a memory. Before long another soul along life's journey appeared just behind him but he gave it no attention and continued on his individual path. Then another and another joined just behind him. The road was not as such to allow other souls to go around. His focus suddenly became less about his journey and more about keeping up in a race that he had not entered. He continued on but lost himself and all he could have learned or experienced from the journey also was lost. This was a familiar but regrettable place. Today he was going to change this pattern and he decided to slow his pace to the point where he was able to just pull of the road and out of the race he had no desire to be in and let the other souls go on. The place he decided to pull off was not special but once there he found it beautiful and serene. The bike, still running with rhythm, his mind and heart opened again to the beauty and lessons of life. As the road cleared he again traveled his own journey. As he went forward he did notice other souls along the road paused, as he had been, or broken and lost. His journey continued but was enlightened by life's miracles and lessons. This journey is my own and I am not obligated to participate in any others he said to himself. The lesson of the day was that sometimes you just need to pull off and follow your own path of time and distance. With confidence and contentment, he rode toward the ominous orange glow of the setting sun, free.

Life challenges us to many quests for answers or solutions. The focus of the pursuit if you're not careful will take you away from what is more important. The people who support and encourage along the way are by far a greater gift than the goal you seek. Take the time and perspective to appreciate those people and make them a part of your life and the initial goal will not seem so important in the overall scheme of things.

Life, can be generous and rewarding and also can be harsh and punishing. There is nothing in life that we deserve. To live it is a gift given to everyone. How you live is absolutely your choice and responsibility. There is no trick or secret strategy. It's simple, the more you give the more you receive. The more you take the more you lose. So those that spend their lives looking for ways to take that which they don't deserve or haven't earned please be warned. That which you take will be taken from you. And to the contrary that which you give will be given to you. We can't allow the haters and takers to distract us from the true Meaning and purpose of life because of fear and regret of actions against us. Have faith in the creator of life and in life itself to bring and restore balance in all things.

I didn't realize how much I missed my best friend until we found each other after a long separation. So long that it felt like a lifetime. Growing up we were always together. If I got in trouble he was there to support me. He shared every good or bad thing that happened in his life and I always felt free and comfortable doing the same. We did not always agree on things but accepted that and moved on. He shared the beauty of life and helped me be more creative. I helped him with discipline and organization. It was like together we were at our best. I have many memories that I take with me forever. Learning to ride that bicycle and then to drive. Our first dates and the first chest hair. Our dreams of the future were very similar and we looked forward to what life would bring. Life happened as they say and that where we drifted apart. At first it was little disagreements but it quickly escalated to the emptiness of total separation. Life continued as always but we remained separate long enough to forget each other. Time passed and I found myself in one of life's many struggles and I was searching for help. I learned to let go of regret and resentment and searched my soul for those things that made me uniquely me. This is when my best friend and I were reunited in a glorious and profound reunion because this also was the time I again realized that my best friend is and has always been me.

Milky is what I imagined as I glanced through my mind. With every color combined without definition or distinction. For the longest time I found this to be my normal. I accepted all things as they were without question or perhaps even awareness. I guess I was happy but I always knew something did not feel right. It was not until I had overcome the fear that I even dared to wonder what the possibilities were. The milky, I realized, was how anything be possible just like a painting with every color combined. They were all there awaiting my wish and command. As I made a choice, it became clear and focused. It is a rare gift to be enlightened to the power and possibilities of my own mind. From caterpillar to butterfly I was transformed, never to be the same. I looked back with sadness upon those things and moments I would leave behind but I knew the precious moments and memories I would carry with me always and they would contribute to the painting of the rest of my life within body and after as a spiritual soul upon the winds of time. Eternally sharing hope and faith to all whom may come after me with the support and oneness of all those before me. Life is a journey with no end but merely checkpoints for growing.

My shoulders grow weak from the constant expectation of weight they carry. My soul has grown tired and weak from the consistent perceived failures. My mind grows tired in the search for answers to bring resolution. Time, I have lost to never be regained. Passion has evolved into disappointment and the only joy I find is in the thoughts of parting. Regrets build and multiply with efforts spent in the achievement of others goals and not my own. When the signs are clearly warning the absence of empathy, why do I continue to pursue. My labor goes unseen and unappreciated even with the occasional achievement. The constant barrage of hate has become overwhelming and transforming. Goals are set as expectations but the failure is always defined as performance related. The concept of setting up for success has long ago been lost and forgotten. Why do the few control the path of the many? Even with my exit from the game it will be played the same. This culture is destined for demise and as it happens we wonder why. I salute the few for their ability to control the many. I do however make it know that I see you clearly and the disgust and hate I carry is by your creation and I hold you accountable for your failure.

Ahead of me the path lay defined by expectations with no distinct origin or validation. Behind me the path lay clearly defined by experience and wisdom. Forward is generally the action taken by most travelers but forward can appear the same depending upon the scale or timeframe we use to review it. There are many branches of our path that we tend to avoid by trying to stay true to the concept of forward. In our life we will have our share of straight, curves, and corners as we allow ourselves to stray from the expected norm. I myself have also lived my life for the most part guided by what I thought was expected of me to do and be. There are also points that we don't any longer believe that we are headed in the right direction and turn around or drift away from where we were headed. When we turn we see where we have been and think it would be a waste to turn and waste all that we have traveled to get here. It was only when I stopped and looked around in all directions that I realized that life is not about a preconceived notion of where we should go or do. Life is about the journey and being free to choose how it may unfold. The true gift is the ability to use where you have been as strength to choose any direction or interest that may appeal to us regardless of the risk or reward. If we are obligated to do anything it is to be the unique individuals we have the capacity of being. Don't regret anything that teaches a lesson and don't settle for anything as the end of the road. Treat every day as an opportunity for the adventure of your life.

powerful and limitless as the mind may be

it is not perfect and often lacks the ability to see

that being hurt by someone with effects long lasting

then unconsciously judging all we meet as masking

the same characteristics we felt from another's hurt

but lack the faith and fairness to be trusting.

Reflection is a word with many different meanings. You look in a mirror and think you are what you see but you see what were. You look in the rearview mirror to see where you're at but you only see where you have been. In your mind you reflect upon a time gone by. All these things are visible to help you look better, learn from wrong places, and utilize the past to help you know what you seek in the future. So, if you're looking in the mirror and see unhappiness, happy times, and everything you own in a small U-Haul, you're going the right direction.

Sadness is enduring and constant without any effort. Happiness on the other hand is temporary and inconsistent and requires great effort. Both of which are states of mind achieved by choice. When a description is given for being sad it usually consists of multiple subjects but an overwhelming I do not know. Happiness on the other hand is very specific and can be defined quickly and completely. Happiness does require choice and action to maintain joy in flight. Sadness however requires nothing as it already lay on the bottom and has nowhere to go but out like flood waters engulf more of our self than was meant to be. Most souls spend much more time trying to discover the reasons they are sad than they do using those things they know make them happy. Would it not make more sense to focus on the certainty of those things that bring happiness rather than dwelling on the search for reasons we are sad? Both are necessary to each other but neither has dominance without our choosing. There are many emotions between sadness and happiness and they are all tools of or souls that help us cope with the many things human life brings. Just because we use a tool does not mean we cannot put it away and use another. God has given us everything we need in this life but will not make us use them. The freedom of choice and how we use it make us who we become. The choice is yours, what will you choose?

The security and hope perceived from the faith in the promise that when one door closes another will open encourages us. For most it falls short because we never truly have the faith to step away from the doorway. We think if we stand in the partially closed doorway that we will be able to see the next doorway opening. The truth is that we must allow the doorway to close behind us in order to move to the next open one. Call it a leap of faith if you will but most people spend their lives standing in the doorway hoping for Devine intervention and vision. Our own actions of faith are required to open new doorways and new opportunities. The support structure is there but one must invoke the effort to enjoy the result.

She spent her days with the anticipation of the setting sun. Each day drawn and painted uniquely and with awe she would absorb the splendor of the sight into her soul. She believed magic of this magnitude could show her the one that would complete her. It was a mate to her soul that she had long wished to discover. She was blessed with abundance of family and friends but the space remained that had yet to be filled. It was a day like the others. She stood surrounded by the majesty of the setting sun. This day was different in that she asked aloud. "Why have you not shown me that which my soul aches for?" tears ran from her eyes from unknown depths. She wiped her tears and then again looked toward the sun but noticed something she had never noticed before. In the background was the faint image of the moon. As she looked closer toward the full moon it became even more glorious. As she marveled at the magic she believed in her mind aroused a thought of someone she knew. Startling her, she heard a voice softly whispering. "I have shown you many times but you were not willing to see". In the distance she saw her friend looking toward the moon. The moment she looked upon him he turned and looked at her. Their eyes locked and each could see through the others with a renewed perspective. Don't get so lost in the search that you cannot see what you search for. May your Valentine's Day offer such enlightenment?

One summer day as a child plays the lessons learned in retrospect become clear as day. In a country setting a child plays along a magically flowing creek. A stick he finds and imagines it to be a ship but not just any ship but one with speed and power abounding. Gently he places his ship within the stream of the creek as it flows long and straight as well as crooked and winding. He imagines being set sail as he closely follows, leads, and travels with his ship as if to race and compete with another. His ship flows well but does on occasion come upon hardships and hazard. he does not remove his ship from danger but gently guides it to safety and allows it to freely continue upon its journey. The boy is traveling always with his creation in hopes of great achievements as he believes in the ships potential. Time and distance continue to climb on the ships journey but the boy never leaves its side. The boy does what he must to keep in pace and as the stream grows wider he even leaps from side to side with the greatest of faith. Impossible or hard are words he does not visualize as remotely relevant to this journey. Twisting and turning, racing and resting, but continuing on his ship does sail and along he stays equally in pace. He imagines and believes to be real that it is he that captains this vessel but yet the role he takes is of support and guidance. His journey sadly comes to an end but still he is there. He sets the ship free but the journey changes from a physical one to that of a spiritual one that guides and comforts the child as he ages and endures but with this lesson never to lose. These lessons be shared with his family and friends and remain in their hearts and soul long after he is gone. God never leaves us and is always guiding us to be people whose impact shall remain in spirit to help those we love as he does for us for all time.

The circumstances were not alone in the view of a house that hoped to be a home. A single room became the entire dwelling. The room was the center of life. The view into the room sees it sparsely furnished but by minimalist definition quite adequate. The rest of this house ceased to exist or serve any purpose. Within the one room was a single window. The window was covered completely from corner to corner. It was not clear if it was covered to push away light or to pull in the darkness. The room with the covered window provided an environment that felt safe and secure. It also was free from judgment and expectation. In this quiet and serene condition, the voices from within were being heard after a long time silenced and disregarded. A room with the symbolism of faith in that no matter what the day might bring it was a place to reconnect with what was truly important. It was a place to get out of the chaos and complications found in a society created by man. Even though the window was covered the view was much clearer and enlightening. We need this place so that we may learn who and what we want to be. We were not created to be that which someone else would have us to be. In the end the room serves as a metaphor for the place within us protected by our faith. It is a view beyond the covered window.

The day awakened bright and warm. The atmosphere was one of clarity and vision. I went forward with the sun having my back and open sky in front of me. Family would join me as the journey began and remain for the entire ride. Friends would also join at various points along the way and some would stay and some would drift away in the direction of their own journey. The signs that came up gave awareness to merging and yields. Offering the addition of new riders on my journey as well the opportunities to yield, recognize and help other on their own journey. Rough road ahead offered insight and the strength found in preparedness and persistence. Construction ahead forced the adjustment of the road traveled but not the destination. Much of the journey was spent with the wind in my face and the warmth at my back. I covered so much ground and made so much progress within these magic intervals. I continued on with the knowledge that the signs would appear again. Speed limit reduced ahead offered the opportunity to slow down and truly appreciate the road marks along the journey. Lane and road changes are many along the way. The loss of family and friends in body brings sadness and times of slowing and reflection but continuing on I must. Forever changed by each gain and loss but with their spirit always guiding me. After time I see the sign stating highway ends. I chose to continue on anyway and I must say that this stretch of the road has been the most enjoyable so far. Those still with me on my journey become even more special and important to me. Those who chose not support my journey and to leave no longer hinder my enlightenment. Even though I know the road will eventually end I look forward to using the stars as my highway. I purposely take the opportunity to relish in these moments as the best so far. The sun still warming from behind and the moon guiding ahead at the same time the stars are visible around me. May you have the faith to read your own signs with equally mesmerizing enlightenment and appreciation.

The day brought with it rain in abundance. The rain was not hard but the soaking and penetrating sort. Nature was happy to be on stage showing off its many colors but hiding the sadness of summer end. The sky at dusk did clear the way for the full moon to take its turn on stage. The streets were empty and lonely. Like a lighthouse in a storm the light from this diner did shine and beckon company. A man, whose life had become one of wandering, did happen upon the glow and draw of the diner. He looked through the window so see scarcely anyone within except one family. He hesitated outside as he had become used to the silence of his own company over time. He was tattered and torn in appearance and most people kept their distance from him. In his heart he knew he was judged by his appearance and not by his content. As he turned to leave, the door opened and a woman similar in age but glowed with the warmth and kindness he had not known for some time. She reminded him of his mother long gone. Come on in honey; get out of the damp and cold evening. He went to speak but the words got stuck in his throat from lack of use. He cleared his throat and told the women he had no money or any way to pay. She looked into the man's eyes and said "no matter". The soul he felt when she spoke those words assured him and made him feel welcome. The diner seemed to be one lost in time. The atmosphere was one of another time. The light within was just bright enough to allows shadows to hang between them. She brought him coffee and the special that was listed on the little chalkboard on the counter. Eat up she said as she gently patted him on the shoulder. There was another family there as well. He assumed this by the young boy's voice in the background. She picked up his plates and refilled his coffee. As he sat there in the warmth of the surroundings a little boy peered above the edge of the table. The little blonde haired and blue-eyed boy reminded him of someone but he could not remember. The boy said hello sir. The woman was behind the counter smiling. His parents were still not seen nor heard. He said hello to the boy and asked him his name. The boy said I am Joshua, who are you? The man had to laugh as he told the boy" Joshua is my name too". The boy climbed into the chair at the table with the man. He then asked the man if he wanted to know a secret. Of course, the man said. The boy said this is a secret of how to see into the future. The man was caught a little off guard. He told the boy that would be a good secret to know. As you can tell by looking at me it would have been helpful earlier in my life. The boy said ok as he climbed to stand on the chair he was sitting in. he reached across the table toward the man. The man leaned back out of habit. The boy said it will be ok. The man then leaned forward toward the boy's outstretched hand. The boy ever so gently extended his finger and touched the man on the forehead. The woman, the whole time standing behind the counter was grinning with an odd look of pride. The boy then said "my mommy says the secret is in here". The man again leaned back in his chair as he contemplated what the little boy had said. Suddenly the thunder crashed outside as the rain returned. The man was startled by the thunder. It felt like the man's entire life flashed before him with the crash of the thunder. His eyes closed as he focused on that story he was seeing. Upon opening his eyes, he heard the woman, Joshua you leave your father be now. In this moment he also realized that he was no longer the tattered and torn man of age. He was the boy. Quickly he responded with a smile to his mother, "yes mommy".

The day was emotionally and physically exhausting. It was a normal day and I fell asleep as quickly as I was able to lay my head down. Of course, falling asleep entailed great conscious effort to relax and release tension noticed in clinched fist and gritted teeth. The dream state does eventually take hold even though I sometimes wish it wouldn't because it takes more from me. In my dream or in my reality depending on your perspective I find myself lost, wandering, and wondering in a dense forest. I sit by the edge of trickling stream and become part of the sound of the water. It is pretty warm, but the slight breeze mixed with the sweat on my forehead make it feel cool and very comfortable. Suddenly a huge white wolf runs past me like I am not even there. It stops just ahead of me and turns to look right at me. Of course, I am frozen with astonishment and disbelief. It then turns away once again and jumps through some trees and seems to just vanish. I anxiously wait for it to show itself again. After I became restless waiting I wander the direction it went. When I get closer I see what looks like a small house or building made with large stones. It looked to have been there long enough for nature to take it back. The trees were from within it and around it. Going even closer I noticed what looked like a doorway with no door. It was black and offered no insight as to what lay within. Even as I stepped to the doorway I could see nothing but darkness within. Curious I took a step through the doorway. I was now surrounded by darkness. I took another step and the doorway vanished behind me. It was like I had just entered another world. It was many times larger than the structure looked to be. There was a bright orange sun shining across a snow-capped mountain upon me. I could feel its warmth throughout my entire body. As I looked away from the sun to see that there is also a glowing full moon casting shadows upon a pale blue ocean. There was a beach with sand as white as the snow atop the mountains. A huge waterfall is filling a stream so clear it looked like a mirror. Just on the bank of the stream I again see the white wolf with must be his family. They looked my way but again looked away as if I belonged there with them. As I looked around and wondered further it did seem this world was filled with things I held sacred. The long and winding blacktop road stretched so far that it looked endless. Everything seemed to be in tune to my wishes and dreams. With no desire to leave I continued my journey of exploration. Again, I see a structure that looked like the one in the forest. Its doorway is nothing but darkness. Just like the other the first step left me engulfed in darkness. The next step the doorway vanished behind me once again. I found myself standing in front of a huge stone wall with some sort of great light shining from behind and all around it. As I looked closer to the wall I noticed writing carved upon it. It said "infinite are the possibilities when infinity is the time frame". As soon as I finished reading it the deafening sound of the alarm waking me for another day of reality, or perhaps fantasy.

The days are dark though the sun shines bright. The nights are clear though the moon cast shadows of blue. She had become so used to existing that she had neglected being. She had become defined by the obligations and commitment she would not deny. Over time the obligations would fade with change but the commitment remained true. True only, in the memory of the initial acceptance. When the obligations give up their light to her commitment she sees not even a sign of that which she committed to at the start. Often, she wonders why she would be punished and why she wouldn't deserve what she has given. Is it possible to commit to a concept and not be held accountable should the concept change? The typical response to her sadness by others is choice. She is guided to make choices that reflect what will make her happy. Regardless of what she may do or not do, the struggle is the internal release from commitment in such a way that her integrity would remain intact. She ignores the truth she knows that integrity comes from within herself and not as perceived by others. Continue on she will with smile through the day until she finds the understanding and acceptance to quiet her restless soul. Until then she will search, explore and even imagine scenario after scenario hidden in the shadows of the moon so blue.

The power to change, to stay, to speak out, to remain silent. We tend to look for these things outside of ourselves. Some spend their lives waiting for signs or instruction. The greatest secret as well as the greatest known truth is that by design the powers of which I speak have and will always lay within us.

The rising sun was forcing its will in the creation of what would be a brilliantly beaming day for the first day of summer. Morning dew dropping from the trees gently awakened a man fast asleep on a bench. He rose to a seat and as he looked upon the spectacle of the day he put his head in his hands and spoke to the morning. God; it's been awhile since I have talked to you and I see by this day you are showing off again. I awaken another day as a lost traveling soul. Help me find my way. He released his hands from his head and uncovered his eyes. It took a moment to again regain focus. When he did he noticed a small boy sitting with him on the bench. The boy was in tattered and faded clothing and looked to be in need. He asked who are you and where did you come from? The boy looked his way but said nothing in return to the man's question. Again, he asked the boy a question. Who are you with and where is your family? This time the boy looked at the man. He placed his little hand over his heart and said; I have no one for everyone I hold dear is within me. The man replied; who talks like that. What is your name boy? The boy replied; you know me as I am. The man laughing at the way the boy talked introduced himself. You know me as Eugene but my mother always called me Eu and so will you. They spent most of that summer wandering together from one place to another. They had many talks and found the joy of many things. Eu did notice that since meeting Iam people seemed nicer and things seemed more beautiful. There were also moments when it was not clear who was leading who. Toward the end of summer, it became obvious to Eu that no one seemed to talk to or even see Iam. Iam, why do people not talk to you? Should you not be in school soon? With warm and comforting eyes Iam said, the need for the school of which you speak has long past. Eu asked of the boy, who talks like that as he laughed. Iam then said; no one can see or hear me but Eu. Again, He laughed at the strange words. Eu pulled the boy close and held him tightly. So tight that your eyes close so tight that tears are pushed into being from the well of joy. Upon releasing Iam he was startled when the boy was no longer there. He looked around franticly in search of Iam with no success. Suddenly a warm and calming voice seemed to appear out of the thin air. You asked for my help finding your way and lesson I bring you is that Iam always with Eu. Peace

The sounds from the track seemed random in the beginning but the longer you listen the more systematic it is. Even more than listening but feeling the rhythm is so calming and relaxing. The windows are open in the car so as you go you can see and smell the areas you pass by from farmland to the flowers in a large meadow. Consistent is the smell of the substance the track is treated with. The way I am dressed somehow feels odd but not sure why. I find myself alone in the car with the exception of a little girl across the aisle gazing out the window and laughing to herself. I shut my eyes for only a moment and as I opened them again the little girl was standing and staring at me. She giggled a little at my surprise but then introduced herself as grace and said she was glad to meet me as she addressed me by name. She seemed to be by herself but I wasn't sure. She took a seat beside me and continued to look out through the window. She saw a beautiful home and asked me if I had one and I responded no but maybe someday. Coming through a town she noticed a couple obviously in love and she asked me if I had someone to love and again I said no but maybe someday. Many places, as we passed she asked, have you ever been there and many times I said no but maybe someday. I hadn't noticed but grace was holding my hand as we were looking through the window on our ride. We began to slow down and grace said this was her stop but I didn't see anything around so I was a little confused and concerned since she was still by herself. As she got up she looked at me as if I was supposed to stop her but I wasn't sure what I should do. She walked to the door and even though I couldn't see anything through the windows I could smell wildflowers and I could hear the sound of water gently flowing and it just felt warm and comforting. As she went to step out the door she turned around and with her hands on her hips she said. It is a pleasure to know you Michael. I am grace, and with the grace of god I remind you that there is no someday. There is only today. Live it. At that exact moment the train whistle blew long and loudly but I soon realized it was my alarm as I awoke to begin another today.

Those things out of our control are many. The beginning and ending of life as we know it are two of the most important. Our beginning we forget and our end we refuse to accept. Neither; follow any set of rules or expectation. As children we are naive and accept all things as possible and credible. At the end we find that there is much more beyond but cannot return to speak of it. It is sad that what we do between is such a contradiction. Perhaps the beginning and end are locked out of our control because we cannot be trusted with it. Perhaps the middle is a test to ensure our appreciation of both. Seems as soon as we become adults by our own determining we start looking for THE ROAD. This road is long and lonely. It lay straight and level. Both sides are partially obstructed with what resembles an early morning fog. In front and behind us we see nothing but the road and the moving dark shadows of others on THE ROAD. This road is created by mankind with a false sense of superiority. Just beyond the fog on both sides is pulsing with brilliant colors and the faint sounds of music and laughter can be heard. You can see the tops of trees swaying in a breeze. You can see the very tops of mountains and only imagine the valleys. The sounds of water remain constant like blood through our veins. The temptation to drift away from THE ROAD is almost overwhelming. The moment we even look we hear the voices saying "stay on the road". The longer we travel on THE ROAD the greater our frustration grows. We regret the miles we have come and we long for what beyond the fog offers us for the rest of our journey or test. We will notice some shadows of those ahead leave THE ROAD. With excitement and apprehension, we watch but they never return. From behind we also catch glimpses of those choosing to venture beyond this road. With each exit we can smell the flowers as the shadow cuts through the fog. Fear again brings back to traveling THE ROAD. Even though we let fear control us, not one of us can truly explain or validate the fear we allow to control us during the only opportunity to enjoy our own control. Each of us is created uniquely and individually by God's hand regardless of how you may interpret it. The true meaning of the test is to see if we can achieve the potential we are given and look forward to what is next. We all are free to choose, but the right choice would be to stop following THE ROAD made by man and follow THE PATH made by God.

To believe that to love is wasted when it doesn't last is the greatest of misconceptions of life. Life and love are about the collection of moments. Those moments may last a life time or they may last a glance. Society tells us of heartbreak and disappointment in love that didn't last as long or as deep as mans assigned expectation. Souls abound with regret and remorse for not finishing the race. Love is not a race but a journey. Love has come to be defined by what we receive when the true purpose of it is in the giving. Relationships may not last but the love you give will change the world forever, and the moments or spans of love you receive change you with validation forever as well. Meet all things with love and cherish all those moments of love you receive. Love is beyond mans practice of defining and we are foolish to think we have the insight that god had when he gave us the ability love and be loved. True insight would be to meet all things along this journey we call life and much closer to gods expectations we may come. Love the journey with peace in your heart.

To take or expect something that is not given freely is to take advantage for selfish and personal gain. It is designed for us to make our own way and only then can we appreciate and deserve that which is given freely.

Under the influence I notice how things are so different. Not just some things but all things are deliciously enhanced. The influence makes wind therapy so much more relaxing. The influence makes the smell of fresh cut grass in the summer so real you can taste it. The influence makes work just work and nothing more. It shows me that the only completion I have is to be a better person today than I was yesterday. The influence allows the sun and the moon to produce colors beyond anything I have ever seen before. Under the influence I find the truth to be very intoxicating. I find the people I know and meet to be such a great blessing. I find relationships are much more in harmony with my true self. Under the influence I become a better listener. I can even hear sounds like the creaks that trees make as they sway back and forth in rhythm to the wind. The power of the sun and the moon penetrate beyond just my skin into my soul. Under the influence I can see my reflection in a mirror and know with certainty that it is only a reflection and not a true image of the soul I carry. Under the influence I have found that anger no longer looms in wait. Anger gives way to love and concern. Under the influence people are much nicer to me and show genuine concern and thus strengthening the desire to be under the influence. Under the influence my mind achieves clarity and vision of what my future holds. It offers me much more satisfaction with acts of kindness than those I might be kind to. Under the influence I find courage and confidence that I never knew existed. I look to the stars as the rain gently caresses my face and I know this feeling must never end. So, to ensure this state for eternity I must forever be under the influence of PEACE.

Under the influence of the light of day the expectation is undeniable and relentlessly beckoning. Even on the cloudiest days the light remains constant in that which it seeks from her. She plays her part in the theater of life. Day by day and moment by moment she perfects the role that must be played. Time as we know it passes and she becomes locked and lost in her portrayal of the part she believes to be expected. Reviews of her performance only come on those days and moments of lost character. The consciousness of society is unaware and unaccepting of anything but the role specific and true. She has convinced herself that far too many depend upon her role for support and example. The role she continues to play but within she hides much sadness and sorrow. She imagines those places and things that bring her comfort and joy. She longs to be free of expectation and free to be honest and true to her inner self. She is so adjusted to the light that when she steps into the darkness neither light nor dark exist. Only after she lingers in the darkness does she achieve clarity and vision. Here in the darkness the theater of life does not exist. She goes to those places she believes are safe and conducive to her true thoughts and feelings. Within the darkness those things of light shine truer than in the light of day. The sound of the ocean tide sweeping in and out. The ocean lay dark blue and endless. The tops of the waves painted white from the reflection of moon glowing down. The warm but very slight breeze comes and goes in rhythm with the tide. The trees gently sway then again rise true. The scents from the ocean and beach meet to mix and emerge unique and soothing. All these conditions combine to provide a placc she can finally investigate and experience her true self. She looks out upon the glory of the beauty in front of her. She can taste the soft, moist and saltiness of dark and blue sea. She realizes the tastes she enjoys are tears from her soul gently trickling down her cheek into the corners of the mouth. She imagines the meaning of her tears and the sea being salty. With clarity she realizes she is part of everything and feels blessed to be a part of it. With this she summons the strength to close her eyes. She closes her eyes and pushes the remaining tears out of hiding and she is at peace until again she wakes.

Unfortunately, familiar is the place we become aware and find ourselves. Our heart says chase your dreams and make them happen but our mind creates a multitude of reasons why we fail. Most times we withdraw and let go of any progress or opportunities and sink back into the sadness of forfeited desires and wishes. All lost out of fear of failing somehow but only after irreversible commitment to the backward journey do we realize time and time again that to try and fail temporarily is by far a greater accomplishment than to never try.

We are all exactly where we are supposed to be right now. However, tomorrow is not known. We exist long enough each day or days or years that it takes for us to learn what we need to know to go forward. Most of the time we know when we need to move forward but we ignore it based on precedents set forth by society and not by god. Many believe it's their destiny they search for but I believe it's the journey that is the blessing. We lose people, we lose things, we lose relationships, but we never truly lose these things as they become a part of us and part of who we have become. The key is to trust god and live by his expectation not mans. no one ever condemns the caterpillar for becoming the butterfly.

We are not, by nature, deserving of all that we want. When we think that we are automatically entitled to something, that is when we start walking all over others to get it.

wrongfully shared but endured we must

now from hate but once from trust

unfairly encountered against our will

judgement awaits as time stands still

lies may deserve an eye and a tooth

but futile it is the weapon of truth

The sun had set long ago. The clouds that were visible during the day now filled the sky like a blanket of shadows. The stars were lost but high in the sky was the moon completely full. A man looking out a window caught the vision and was uncontrollably compelled. Out under the moon he walked. The night was silent except for the hum of the moon shining so brightly like the electrical wires stretched across a tower. He wondered why and how that only the moon could shine through the clouds that obscured all other things. As he walked toward the moon it seemed to retreat and lead him on further and deeper into its trance. Every step he took made a deafening sound against the stillness of the night. He tried to walk more cautiously in hopes of softening the noise he was making. Finally, he just stopped and when he stopped so did the moon from its retreat. The mesmerizing hum now became loud enough that he could feel the hair stand upon his arms. His eyes closed and the vision became even clearer. Not just the sights and sounds but he felt everything was in a heightened state of clarity. It is not known how long he remained but he did revisit often with the knowledge he had gained by the experience. Do not let yourself be the noise that keeps you from hearing or seeing what is important with passionate vision.

A moment paints a picture of a lazy summer day. A man's voice surrounded by the voices of children can be heard in the distance. Closer we look to see the man sitting on his porch and the children intently listening with their eyes. He was telling stories and filling in the colors as each child would ask a question in turn based on their own unique perception. The moment brought times of silence and awe and also laughter so infectious. From the distance the exact words could not be heard but picture being painted under the sunny summer sky was beautiful and unique to all willing to see it. In a silence not like the others a woman's voice could be heard. Her voice was much clearer because of the volume she spoke. After she urged the children to go home she turned her attention to the man. "Why do you insist on telling these kids all this stuff? You know they are not true and no one believes you". He was silent but looked upon the woman with his eyes so blue. As she starred at him waiting on a response she felt herself being drawn into the man's world through his eyes. The moment she realized and resisted the temptation he responded. "Truth is merely a perception and I do not seek their belief. I merely remind them where the door is so that they can find it if they choose when they are where you are". She stormed off but his words in that moment would remain.

I could hear the train coming from afar. I knew it wasn't within sight but I still looked toward the track that lay in front of me. I was home and the track was at the end of the road. Of course, I didn't see the train but I did see someone walking on the track toward the train. I didn't give it much thought since the train was still some good ways off. I looked again and they were still there but standing still. Again, I dismissed it even though I thought it was strange. It was one of those days that I became lost in my own little world. Of course, answers never came or at least I didn't see them if they did. The horn of the train awakened me from my state of self-pity. It was close now and as I looked toward the track and they were still there walking again toward the train. Anxiety was directing me at this point so I began walking toward the track. As I got closer I could see it was a man. He did not appear to even now the train was coming. Again, the horn sounded loudly and escalated my walk to a run. I ran as fast as I could because he was not moving at all. I yelled out to him in warning but the train horn drowned the sound of my voice. The moment I reached him and we both fell from the track from the force of my run the train also passed by us. I looked to see if he was alright but he was not there. He must have got up and left as I was regaining my bearings. After the train had completely passed I was greeted by a neighbor asking me if I was alright. I asked her "did you see where he went"? She said "who?" I said "The man on the track". Again, she asked me if I was alright and I assured her that I was. She said "the only person I saw on the track was you but I'm glad you were able to save yourself". I looked up and ask her "save what?" she said "I couldn't get there and I'm not sure I could have done anything so I'm glad you were able to SAVE YOURSELF".

He willingly accepted the commitment of building something that would last forever. It would be something that would take much time and strength. The stones used were heavier in the beginning but remained significant in weight throughout. Unforeseen setbacks became just part of the process. His life became that of carrying stones one after the other and day by day. The vision and the commitment of completion was surely a passion. The compromises and sacrifices were great but would be well worth it. Then one day he was told that his efforts were not good enough. There was nothing he could change or adjust to make it acceptable. Someone else was already working on something that was more acceptable and desirable. For the longest time he just stood there holding a stone trying to understand. Eventually he laid down the stone and walked away. He was told "go build something else new and to your own specifications".

As he tried to begin again he found himself unable to carry the stones. He soon realized that he was so used to carrying the weight of the previous project that though he laid them down, the weight was still upon him. Adding additional weight was just more than he could bear. In time the weight of the prior obligation would lessen and disappear. It became as laborious to release himself of that weight and he knew he would not be strong enough to start anything new until then. Never would he be the same but someday he would be free again.

Late one night after work I went to Walmart. I preferred to go late and avoid as much congestion and noise as possible. As I made my way up the isles I guess I was in too big of a hurry and kept looking behind to see the isle labels. Out of nowhere I was startled as I ran into the cart of another shopper. It was an elderly lady and she had blue hair. She had the kindest smile as she looked at me as I apologized. As her smile retracted again I was startled as she spoke to me. Her voice sounded like that of some sort of demon. Her voice did not even come close to her image. In this demonic voice she screamed at me "LOOK WHERE YOU ARE GOING, NOT WHERE YOU HAVE BEEN, DAMMIT". Then the kind smile returned as she made her way down the alcohol isle. I just stood there stunned. Part of me wanted to respond but the better part of me couldn't deny her point was valid.

He was walking a path that he was accustomed too. From a distance he could see something strange that he had not seen before and without even thinking the fear of the unknown was growing within him. Slower and slower he walked as it became more into sight but clarity of definition or understanding remained lost. As he came close enough to hear that there was some sort of life within, it remained still. SUDDENLY AND VIOLENTLY it sprang into movement. The razors slashed across his face and fear consumed him. He tried to run but met with resistance. He screamed from the pain and fear. The pulsating light and thunder surrounding seemed enhanced by his fear. Whiteness fell like rain and the dark liquid pooled and spread consuming everything around it. After consumed it would continue to drip and stream from every crack and crevice. Without any warning a paralyzing and blinding light burned brightly from above. All became silent except the even more pronounced sound of the dark liquid continuing to consume. He just lay there frozen and vulnerable. As she slowly raised her head from her hands the teacher said "oh my god goodness". "Great job Timmy". "I am sure your dog and your new kitten will get used to each other and we arc all sorry that it ruined your movie night". "Now class, who would like to go next to tell a story of home"? IS PERCEPTION REALITY?

Life's journey is one of rejection. Rejection itself diminishes and denies the courage required to reject anything that creates conflict within the mind, body, and soul. Life is then, a puzzle of conflicts.

Bridges metaphor of life some old and some new

Some require a price in anticipation of the view

Some give the view as validation of price to be due

Some make one wonder if the perception of free is true

One may be plain while another adorned with lights of blue

Covered ones appear like a tunnel that you must travel thru

Suspended and open ones instill a fear of whether safety is true

They all lead you from somewhere old to somewhere new

Regardless of the direction of travel chosen only by you

It is said that burning a bridge can avoid paying the high price due

From a place where you believe a debt may still be due

But to burn one bridge would you not have to burn all others too

The solution would be to suggest that each bridge renders a clue

And would be better left intact as a resource for growth anew

So, all the views collected contribute to a truer more passionate you

As I contemplate the concept of faith always involving risk I find that I may quickly agree but ultimately disagree. Risk is a state of action based upon a perceived or desired result. Faith is a state of mind, or state of reaction if you will, based on a state of being that allows one to accept the outcomes of our every action. Risk is any possible result from our actions that do not meet our perceived expectations. Risk does not evolve from not experiencing the desired result but from the perceived undesired result. A man who expects to fly before he jumps off a building experiences risk but a man who expects to fall faces no risk. Faith allows one to always find the positive from every outcome or action. Faith will bring joy of success or it will bring a lesson contributing to our growth. Faith is a place of comfort in knowing that all things happen as they are designed regardless of our individual perceptions. It is having faith that all goals can be achieved or knowledge will be gained and the goal can change. Faith is a trust in a higher power and risk is the absence of it.

Those early morning expectations can seem extreme until in reflection you realize that each and every one places you in a front row seat to the dawn of the day. Your faith in humanity can be rescued from that place of safety that it has been forced to hide. You can come upon a few souls uniquely blessed individually and compounded exponentially as a group. Together they create an environment where it can feel comfortable again to remove the heavy coat of protection. Skepticism quickly gives way to the enjoyment and appreciation of the trueness and potential of the human spirit. Genuine care and concern can be found sometimes and can provide those moments that build and reinforce the character of our own souls. These by chance opportunities come about as each of us travel our own journeys of repair and renew. We can be tenacious in the belief that healing must happen before we can travel forward. This belief can be challenged as we are made aware of a somewhat different road. Healing is a must but it doesn't serve our best interest to wait on it. It makes more sense and serves us better to change into that coat of who we will become and heal within it. This process will allow a uniquely individual process and reduces the resistance we face by waiting. Souls who can illuminate us without any expectation other than the growth of our Wellbeing will forever remain a cherished moment. As the spirit I pay forward I acknowledge and express appreciation. Onward I travel encouraged and inspired to find the light within all encounters, even if only a dentist appointment.

The glass rattles ever so slightly as you touch the door. A creak of age quickly gives way to the jingle of a bell. Only one jingle then silence as the door opens widely. The smell was that of a very old book but before you could fully see the smell you will feel the still open door waiting patiently for you to close it. The bell and then the creak of age warn of your presence. Once closed you find yourself looking through the rattling glass of the door. Everything that can be seen looks like a black and white photograph covered in smudges and fingerprints from many years of reflection. The old book smell regains your attention and fascination. Visions of stories and writer's perceptions are conjured from the aromas. The light was dim and seemed to come only from the flickering oil lamps strategically placed throughout. The interior was made up of old and heavily oiled woods. There are old photographs on the walls from ceiling to floor. They seem to reflect a wide array of interests, art, and culture. They line the stairways to the many levels within. The silence looms with a sense of sadness. There is no one o been seen but there are signs of recent activity all around. On a counter there is one of those bells you touch to ring with an engraved plaque in front of it. The letters on the plaque are precisely painted to fill what was lost with the engraving. Each letter was just a slight shade darker red than the one before it. Touching the bell, you quickly realize that it no longer rings, even if perhaps it ever did. It makes no sound and gives no warning. With disappointment she turns back to the door with anticipation of the jingle. She stops momentarily in the silent stage of the door before leaving. The oil lamps are flickering frantically now from the breeze the open door allows. She pulls the door closed and turns to be blinded momentarily by the colors of light focused upon her. Slowly her eyes refocus and adjust. I walking away the words of the sign still challenge her. The words read "ring only if you offer equally that you wish to receive".

Were they destined to spend eternity chasing one another or is it merely a moment that they run. From the desserts bland to the oceans rich they roam. They touch the top of the highest mountain and fill the lowest valley. They can make snow piercingly bright or bring water to a glorious blue. They can bring such light to one world then quickly show the lights of others. Are they lovers chasing dreams or exposing them as a team. Seemingly forever locked between the attraction and realization. One pulls the softness of the world's waters only to return them as tears. The other pushes and pulls at the culmination of those tears as if trying to take them away. Their dance will create life and energy and then provide rest and renew. This portrait painted as a love story of two lovers forever existing as a beginnings passion and an endings vision. Constantly they tease with the questions of truth and definition. They bring the front row to its feet in anticipation as they appear illuminated as a union. But alas it is only momentarily. It is in this moment we fall witness beyond comprehension. The moment when the sun will blink and the moon will blink.

The winds of time blew gently upon his face and he knew his turn had come. Armed only with his perception of readiness and the pictures painted for him as expectations the journey began. Quickly he would find his perception to feel false but the expectations unfolded so vividly true. His world would evolve absent of color but clearly defined as black or white. Many moments he would encounter and enjoy but continue on looking for the precise definition. Definitions he found not from within but from comparison to the expected vision he carried with him. Failure finally emerged as regret as he spent as much of his journey looking back as he did forward. There came a point where he no longer believed in the expectation and began to put more faith in those visions of his own soul. Those visions led him away from the well-traveled path to one of his own choice and creation. In that instant of self-awareness, the colors of the universe cascaded around him in warmth and comfort. The once dense forest that surrounded him gave way to a wide and gently flowing valley. The demon of regret was still present but each time with less strength. Open to possibilities beyond his current imagination but attainable he ventured on. Led by his own soul he found his perception was no longer limited and he could see the beauty in all things. Regret would fade entirely away and was replaced by the faith that there are no mistakes but merely lessons. These lessons would enrich and enlighten the soul he would become. That which we become is merely the education to become what we will be.

Upon the road we all must travel there are many signs and warnings. Similar to the blacktop highway we ride but traveling all the same. For the most part we follow and accept without hesitation any and all signs along the journey of the body. The color orange can sway us from our path of comfort without even a word of suggestion. The danger of ignoring the signs paints its picture in our minds and without fear or resistance we change or alter our course. The journey of the soul on the other hand is just the opposite. We tend to ignore any and all signs warning of change. The road of this journey can hit rough places as well as impassible places but we refuse to alter our path. Again, the danger the signs represent are clear but these we ignore or deny. It would ultimately seem we have more faith in man's creation than we do in man's creator. Next time you see the orange cones I challenge you imagine the metaphor.

The darkest of clouds are not always visible but they are always there. They await the conditions which bring them energy and power. You can consciously try to avoid them but ultimately, they are an integral part of life. You can spend your life wasting the clouds of white regretting having ever being consumed by the darkness. It is in the realization that all things are connected will you come to discover that dark clouds offer regeneration and nutrients for growth. The regret and avoidance of such blessings is such a contradiction of their intended purpose. Labels placed on this type of behavior only have power if you believe and that is our choice. Dark clouds are a metaphor for an opportunity for reorganization and refocus. Even our creator utilized a day of rest along the path to perfection. Embrace the darkest of moments for what they are designed for. They are the opportunity to gather the energy of life within you and reach even greater levels of growth in the light. You can be in the light and suddenly become surrounded by the dark clouds and you find it difficult to walk. You can look back at your footprints and they will not look true to your soul. That is because in those moments God is also walking in our shoes to bring us through. In his image we do the same thing with our own children. We let them walk on their own but when they struggle we carry them until once again they run. Choose the belief that sets you free.

Even in the darkness he continued to travel. He would travel upon the tracks of comfort and familiarity. So accustomed to the path he failed to even notice nature's progression in reclaiming. As his mind wandered something made him look behind one day. Far away in the distance was light seemingly following him. It seemed so far away that he gave it very little attention and continued on. Once again, the urge to look back overcame him. This time the light was much closer and a piercing blue with a halo of grey. This time the fire of fear was stoked within him. He began to walk faster thinking he might reach his destination before the light would catch up to him. He wasn't sure of his destination but he thought he must be close given the length time he had been traveling. The soft rumblings of awakening behind him now pushed his pace to a run. Once again, he turned to look behind him and the light was almost upon him and he could feel the heat on his back. Panic was now taking the place of fear. He no longer believed his destination would come and he was running to fast to see nor seek any opportunities off the path he was traveling. One last time he looked behind and the moment he turned the piercing blue light and the heat and the rumbles of awakening overtook him. The force pushed him from his run to a tumbling upon the ground. In the fall his glasses were thrown from his face and as his body came to rest he lay there with his eyes closed. The heat and the light were burning through his eyelids. He summoned the courage and opened his eyes to look upon that which had captured him. The light was so bright he was only able to open his momentarily but that moment released a vast array of colors like he had never seen nor imagined before. The heat was overwhelmingly calming as he explored the colors and wonder of the momentary vision. As he stood up he again open his eyes and he found himself in an open green meadow. In the distance the trees were swaying and stretching from the heat. The sound of water gently running and the meadow grass was magically painting pictures like a hand across velour. All the colors he had seen were now painted randomly upon everything around him. His blue lensed sunglasses were lying on the ground in front of him. He reached to pick them up but stopped just short and let them lay. Again, he looked back at the rising sun and he wondered if it was ever about a destination or was it always about a journey.

Only within obscurity would she ever allow emotion to taste the freedom of escape. The caged environment in which she held them served only to magnify their power as they relentlessly sought release. The perceived sign of weakness she was diligent to not express. The constant and building pressure of her unreleased and unexpressed emotions would become an effort of such distraction that she could no longer even imagine a life beyond them. One day after another she would play the role she had chosen for herself. One day in her daily struggle of pretense she found herself caught within a cool spring rain. At first, she ran to escape the rain but after reaching a point where it became clear she would not escape she slowed to a walk. At first it was so cool that it shocked her senses but soon became like a blanket of comfort. She looked up into the falling drops with a courage she had forgotten even possessing. As the drops of water blanketed her face and ran down her cheeks she felt a release of the prisoners she carried with her. As she stood still in the pouring rain she acknowledged to herself. "If nature could be the strongest of creations and it could rain tears then she would not be weak in doing the same." In a violent surge similar to a dam breaking she set her emotions free. Her tear drops flowed along with rain drops and blended into one emotional release. What she felt was the longest time she stood there in release was truly only a moment in time. But in that moment, she discovered a truth beyond society's labels and would walk every step of her continued journey changed and enlightened. She was already an encourager but now she could passionately encourage you to seek the truth within each and every moment of life.

She was working away but appeared lost in thought. Her thoughts were disrupted by the sound of a familiar voice but she dismissed it quickly. Again, she heard the voice saying "what is it little girl?" the voice was a stranger beside her. Startled and confused by the question and the familiarity of the voice she simply replied "hello" to him. She then asked him if she could help him with anything. He responded "no, but can I help you? What occupies your thoughts little girl?" Maybe it was the familiarity or perhaps the calming tone of his voice but she felt oddly comfortable as she told him what was occupying her mind. "I need to have more confidence and I am not sure how to do that". He pulled out the chair beside her and encouraged her to sit beside him. "Let me tell you something little girl. We are all born with all the confidencc we will ever need and it can be witnessed by all children. Our tree of life has a core of confidence and its care and growth lay in our hands. In time we can, by choice, hang ornaments of doubt upon our own tree. Too many ornaments can weigh down the branches and hinder its growth and potential. The key is to take responsibility for our own tree with the same passion we show for others. So, when you say you need to be more confident I say you are wrong, you need less doubt. The only limits to what we can do or be lay within our own mind and are our choice. Take down those ornaments of doubt and set yourself free." Suddenly she was called away and she excused herself. A few steps away she turned to thank him for his words but he was not there. The table where she sat with him was empty and undisturbed other than the two chairs pulled away from the table. She asked where the man went that was sitting there and was told that the only one sitting there was her.

The miracle of birth brings also with it the automatic and immediate participation in the relay run of life. Each entry is as important as those who entered before and behind us. It begs to be defined as a race but it is more accurate to be defined as an exploration of growth. Early on we do not truly recognize the impact of passing by another soul. It is not until later that we feel the impact and profound sadness as we realize that those we passed came from before us or even behind us. And the longer we go the more we pass by those before us. There is no winning or losing but only a continuous spiritual growth. Walk your own path and pace and find happiness and appreciation for those things we might race by now and miss the opportunity completely. Take the time to feel a sunrise. Embrace the love of family and friends. Absorb the knowledge and growth of those before and behind you. The true purpose and goal is to gain, share, and pass on only those things that can be carried with us forever and shape the world in which we exist. Consider the merit of the baton as you pass it on.

Many times, he walked to the edge and looked beyond it. Many times, he wanted to make the leap but fear prevented the effort every time. The fear of not being able to make that leap and falling into the nothing below was overwhelming and strong. He knew that he should appreciate what he was surrounded by on this side but deep within he knew his journey was meant to follow that path he imagined on the other side. One day as he stood at the edge dreaming and hoping the day would bring the courage to travel on. Suddenly the momentum of sadness from behind reached just enough power to push him over the edge. As he fell he turned to see the sky. The sky reminded him of his beliefs and trust in a greater power. Just as suddenly as he was made to fall he landed in the edge. It was filled with green of grass and flowers of colors he had yet to even imagine. Immediately he wondered if this were heaven but as he sat up he saw a path before him leading to his continued journey. As he looked up to the sky again he would notice the cliff that many times he had stood wishing but fearing. He wondered why he had never noticed this passage before from the edge but knew it was because he was never meant to see it. Faith does bring risk but the risk comes from failing or refusing to imagine the possibilities it can bring you.

Every morning for about a week a bird would make noise just outside the window. It was early and before I needed or wanted to awake. At first, I would pull the blanket over my head hoping to drown it out but it only got louder. Then I tried turning the radio up but again it was over shadowed by the bird's chant. Then I turned the fan on high but still no relief from the unwanted disturbance. Then I just started getting up when the bird would sing but that didn't stop it from singing. What was it doing and why? The end of the week I was again awakened by the song which seemed to grow in volume each day. This day I felt I had had enough and I went to the front door. Perhaps if I went outside I could scare it off and it would leave me alone. Storming to the front door I went. I opened the door and was immediately greeted by the glowing heat and the blinding colors of the sunrise. It was beautiful beyond measure and my angered state quickly evolved to one of melancholy and understanding. We are all one and because we tend to think we are superior and individual we miss or ignore the signs directing us upon the beauty and tranquility of life. It was a moment in which I would forever be changed and enlightened by the connection all things share. I never heard the bird again after that but I look for the sunrise and sunset everyday no matter what I may be doing or wherever I may be. It is humbling to realize and believe you can be part of something so magical and it is reassuring to realize and believe that it is part of you. Open yourself to the possibilities and relish the opportunities.

The day shined brightly with another unique sense of anew. The sea was calm enough to walk upon and the wind blew ever so gently but just enough to sail forward. The silence of the barely filled sails offered a welcomed concentration of thoughts and dreams. In the distance was a cloud, resembling those that filled the sky with cotton. This cloud was like the others but seemed to be resting upon the stillness of the sea. No matter what change in direction was made the cloud stayed just ahead and unavoidable. The gentle winds made movement toward the cloud slow and seemingly deliberate. The slowness allowed the mind to imagine its existence for the good as well as the bad. As his vessel entered into the cloud the wind vanished and his sails fell to leave him adrift within the cloud. Inside the cloud he found it to be similar to being in a fog. The moistness of the fog he could feel upon his face and the taste of the salt water was strong. He waited in silence as he contemplated over and over what he should do if anything. Suddenly from all around him a voice beckoned to him. "To travel on I offer you three choices. You must pick one as no choice will leave you here forever. Choice one is to go back in time and hope to avoid where you are now. Choice two is to give up here and cease to exist. Choice three is to risk that which may lie ahead of you. What will you choose?" he pondered the three choices as well as the warning of not choosing. Was there another choice he could not see or was he destined to choose one of the three offered? The voice remained silent waiting and cloud only seemed to surround him more densely with the passing of time. Summoning the courage, the sailor acknowledged the voice. "I choose number three as it is the only one that I can control. Slowly the cloud disappeared and again he found himself moving forward powered by the gentle winds. Again, he heard the voice but this time from within himself. "You have chosen wisely my son."

The battle was one that would eternally rage. It takes many shapes and forms but it always comes down to fighting for what you believe. After many such battles a large army can be reduced to only a handful or maybe even one or none. One such army over time had been reduced to only a handful. There number did not affect the strength of their belief. The day came that they were pitted against a much larger group whose sole purpose was to defeat them in battle and in doing so bring validation to that which they believed and wished to force everyone to follow. As they stood at opposite ends of large field it became very clear they were greatly outnumbered and their success seemed unlikely. One of the soldiers of the small group stepped forward and began to throw off any armor he was wearing for protection. He stood facing the larger foe with only his sword and passion for what he believed. One by one the rest of the smaller group did the same. The large army watched as grew even more confident of their pending success. The small and passionate group made their charge, as the larger hesitated in disbelief but did eventually move forward. It soon would become evident that the larger army was mistaken in their confidence. The larger army was a trained and experienced group but their training involved an armed and protected army. They were confused and disoriented and found their training not sufficient in dealing with an opposing army armed only with a sword and their belief and faith as armor. One by one the larger army would be reduced and one by one the smaller army's faith grew stronger and stronger. The small group would find victory this day but the victory was only drawn from the right individuality. They did not celebrate but instead mourned the loss of life. They knew the ultimate battle would never end and even though not today the day would come for them to perish. But to perish would only be another beginning and they may be conquered physically but their faith and passion would ensure their invincibility spiritually.

You can tell when Mother Nature is trying to seduce and summon spring to her side. She wears her best perfume that fills the air with colors of dogwood. She teases and taunts him with the sunshine and her warmth and passion. It is usually a tough and long-awaited reunion. Spring is like many of us as he gets hurt with the rejection felt when she chooses another season to walk beside her. Again, in many ways like us which makes sense since we are all one energy. She is relentless in her pursuit and though sometimes it takes longer than others eventually spring remembers the love that stays within him and joins her. Winter being even more the jealous lover will fight to the end and will remain as long as the opportunity may present itself. Spring knows full well that she will soon turn her interest to summer but life is about moments. With this knowledge and understanding all the seasons, glorious in their own way, challenge the rejection over and over again. But in the end, it all becomes worth it just to share the moments in time that transcend the concept of possession. Spring may be loyal and trustworthy but always the jilted lover he shall remain. Find your own encouragement as you play witness to each season's display of talent and miracle never ending.

It's impossible not to stare but the line runs thin between staring and attraction. The latter is uniquely more appropriate. Her dark eyes capture you and pull you in without mercy. When you struggle to free yourself, and succeed all you can wonder is why. Her long dark hair ended in gentle curls. Each one more perfect than the other. She walks with such grace that it seems air itself steps aside so as to not disturb perfection. She seats herself and her legs cross before resting. She slips off her shoes to expose her bare feet gently crossed. As she eats she looks to enjoy each bite like nothing she may have enjoyed before. Her joy expresses itself even through her bare feet as she extends and arches her food with each morsel she would consume. Consumed it exactly what emotion she arouses by her mere existence. Then as suddenly as she controlled you she slips away with the stern look from the man across from her. But it too late as you have already intimately experienced the beauty within her.

In a moment of courage, he opened the blinds and let the sun shine through. As the sun gave a uniqueness and beauty to everything around him he wondered. With grateful anticipation another moment led him to raise the blinds and allow the power to engulf him with its entirety. He stood there cloaked only in the warmth of God's eyes. Nowhere did he see judgment or condemnation. The realization of safety and support drove him to door. With a strong, confident, and supported hand he turned the knob quickly and threw open the door. Any remaining insecurities vanished as the breath of God completed the armor found first of the eye's. A series of thoughts suddenly came to light as if they were placed there purposely. No one had any power over him unless he gave to them from within himself. One step and one moment at a time he went forward courageously and confident. Faith in the armor he wore was all he needed no matter what he may encounter along his continued journey. The blinds and the door behind him remain open but only now as a reminder of accomplishment and another book in the library of wisdom. Even when things may grow dark the Son remains with us in the illumination of the moon. His journey continues today still, as the soul within us.

With every moment of distance, we travel beyond a comfort zone adds yet another piece to the puzzle that is our hopes and dreams.

A self-proclaimed king of only one mirrored image grew old in the blink of passing time. As he sat looking out upon the kingdom he called his own he pondered many mysteries. Confident in his own strength within but no challenge had ever breached his armor of faith. Caring of heart and few seemed worthy only to be dismissed upon the foundation of not being in the same place as he. Treasures had come and gone but never did they satisfy the desire to defeat the loneliness. The walls of his defense were high and strong. So much so he often reflected in awe of how he could accomplish such a task. Perhaps much too late but still he did realize that being in the same place as he was not a defining trait with much importance. Different places allowed for a genuine sharing and learning union. He also came to realize that with walls so high he could not be seen or heard. But still he remained out of sight waiting to be seen but it was never to be a realization. The crack of thunder roused him from his pondering state and he felt the coolness as well as the sting of the rain as it fell upon his face. He stepped back within his perfect wall made up of many imperfect stones. The storm continued relentlessly and so persistently that the imperfect stones of his walls foundation would loosen their grip. Fearing a collapse, he knew he must attend to his wall. As he envisioned where first he would start and stepped toward that direction a great ray of light from the sun did shine directly into his eyes. As he shielded his eyes he would see the most defined rainbow he had ever seen. As he gazed upon its beauty his fear of wall collapse lost its hold upon him. The rainbow seemed to start and end in the same place. That place was upon him and as he allowed himself to believe his perception would forever change his life. Perfection is the collaborative effort of imperfections. His wall fell around him but he stood taller than he had ever stood before and his voice and presence echoed across the merely borrowed kingdom.

After much internal jousting for importance she was ultimately moved to step in one of two directions. Loneliness and heartache meant she would step beyond the obscured veil of protection that would ensure her independence and solitude. From here she became vulnerable to the desire to be shared by another. The opportunity for a soul mate exponentially increased and would satisfy the constant desire and craving. But to be and share a soul mate requires a blending and thus involves giving away some of the solace enjoyed with solitude. The other direction would be to step back even further behind that veil and eliminate any chance or choice of losing the silence but also diminished the opportunity to let go of the loneliness that would at times consume her. Often, she wondered if a balance could exist and allow her to enjoy and find happiness in both. A woman of age was sitting on a bench within a cloud watching her step in and out over and over. She, with raised voice, said for the world to hear. "It would seem to me that your mind is strong and secure. In being selfish you are denying your heart the chance to discover it greatest potential. Your misguided fear of losing that which can never be taken is keeping you from allowing your heart to do the same. As the woman of age threw her hands up in the air as an example of her waning patience, the veil disappeared.

I gazed through the window, covered metaphorically, without any agenda or goal. As I wandered the many paths and possibilities I gently fell into a state of dream within a dream. It was here that I found myself walking in a lush garden illuminated by endless colors of a setting sun and the ominous glow of a rising moon. The union of color and glow painted the garden with brush of pastel. In the distance I could see extruding from the middle of everything a large and towering tree. The tree with its large base any many branches seemed to touch everything as the tree of life. The path, lined with pastel flowers, led to and from the tree just as the many other similar paths I could see. A swing was hanging from one of the trees strong limbs and in the swing, was a couple swinging back and forth in the gentle breeze. They acknowledged my presence and waved warmly and true. Without even thinking I waved back as I continued the path which was leading me closer to them. Once close enough I greeted them and asked where we were. They responded "we are here, there, and everywhere". I told them the name I go by and asked theirs. The woman spoke first saying her name was faith and then the man told his name to be courage. Sensing my slight confusion by their names, Faith said "we walk together forever and always". Courage continued her thought by saying, "It takes faith to have courage and it takes courage to have faith". They invited me to sit with them upon the swing. As I sat next them I could feel the warmth and power of their union as the swing continued swaying in the breeze without any effort of my own. Silently I sat there with faith and courage swinging back and forth on the tree of life. A feeling of comfort and belonging overcame me like nothing else I had ever felt. Forever changed by a dream within a dream. Or was it?

Bridges exist and serve both real and metaphoric purposes along the roads of life. Some will avoid them and some will burn them. Some cross them back and forth many times and never get very far from them. Some are visionaries and build them as needed in whatever direction they wish to go. Some are so small that one can cross in a blink and some so large one could lose patience waiting to completely cross. Some are old and comfortable and some are new and mysterious. Even with all the travels and bridges of life very few ever notice that the best view of a sunset or sunrise comes when you are in the middle of a bridge. So, when you imagine a bridge a something to get from one place to another now I hope you will imagine a bridge as something to lift us up and away from ourselves and offer an improved perspective.

Every day enticed by the rising sun a little more than the day before. Promises and teases of limitless color created finally a traveler upon the world. Free of burdens and weight to carry made the mountains easily conquered. The journey did lead far from the physical and spiritual beginning. In time came the discovery of a lush and green valley. The valley represented everything that was expected to be found. Here the traveler would rest with the expectation of forever. In time the sunrise that led this journey would change and leave the lush green valley in darkness. Little by little the valley would turn dry and grey until the entirety of this home fell into darkness. Pushed to the edge the traveler found two choices from which to choose. Travel on seemed impossible because of all there was to carry. The load made the mountain that lay next too hard to conquer. To remain would mean to continue on in the darkness and death of what once was. The now cold and emptiness experienced in remaining would soon steal all hopes and dreams that once flourished vividly. Now alone and surrounded by all those things and thoughts carried the traveler grew weak and insignificant. It was in the act of giving up and letting go in hopes to cease existence that answers were provided. With each item let go made room for new and gave the soul strength to travel on. To carry everything is pointless. Carry only those things that nourish and know the journey is never over.

A man who can observe and realize the darkness mankind practices with only the emotion of finding it funny carries the ultimate hope within him. He can watch as people judge one another by how they look, what they wear, or even perhaps by the car they drive. His belief is strong of the soul being the only thing that portrays trueness. He accepts everyone with the trust of a child. This trust is something most will lose as they venture upon the world and succumb to the pressure of belonging to the majority group. The group governed by prejudice. The times are very sad when we show respect based on the illusion of implied wealth. True wealth dwells in our mind and heart and never seeks to draw attention to its existence. A man who can find it funny without any anger or desire is truly one of few. Faith can be found in one courageous man willing to walk against the winds of society. Wind is changed by resistance. Where will you stand in the wind?

As with all travelers of time, the choice of where and when is free. The most common choice is the past. When the mind and soul choose the past, they encourage the body to follow. Sometimes the body resists but has no influence over the mind and soul. Sometimes the body will go along. As they approach those many things that might spark the sensations of past the body will be the only one to feel the fear deep within. The fear of seeing or coming into contact with that past that was unkind. The true realization is that when we encounter the past we always envision it with resolution. In that resolution it changes from the past to something that did not or perhaps has not happened. This form would be better defined as the future. A future strengthened by wisdom. Even though travel to the past is most common, we fail to recognize or understand that the past is the foundation for the future. This being said it would make sense to say we never really travel to the past but always the future. Things that happened behind us can only be changed in front of us. Travel on. Travel often. Travel with peace.

Without any warning, other than a feeling in the air and the look of possibility, it came upon me. At first, I reacted with a resistance surely born of society conditioning. It became obvious very quickly that escape was unattainable. It was then that I altered my perception from one of reaction to one of response. The sting of contradiction evolved into a warmth of acceptance. It welcomed me without prejudice as if I have always been connected to something so much larger than my own individuality. Any expectations I may have had would drown quickly in the ocean of life's aura. Within those moments of release, I would find a much greater power on which to hold tightly through all things I would encounter from the past or future. As I became drenched in the blanket of support and comfort that it freely offered I found strength within waiting to be discovered. Eternally changed I now walk with anticipation of the next moment of enlightenment like the one I found in a morning spring rain.

The vender mall was crowded with people. After many attempts this day brought the environment she felt confident to enter alone. Like a ghost she wandered throughout. Many items of age and unknown stories she would admire and softly touch imagining the story. Some things that drew her interest were being viewed one of the many around and she was forced to wait her turn. The indirect path she would take awaiting her turn at the item of her interest would lead her to other treasures she probably would have never even noticed had her journey not been disrupted. In her wandering she came upon a place off the beaten path. Immediately catching her eye was a mirror exuding beauty and history. As she examined the workmanship and decoration first she knew that was to summon the courage to look upon the mirror. From habit as she did look into the mirror she looked only into the reflection of her own eyes. As she looked into her own eyes soon she noticed her eyes held the reflection of her standing before the mirror. Once that hurdle of self-esteem was cleared she looked upon her face as it would reflect from the mirror of a time gone by. She reached out to touch her face in the mirror and when she did she felt the soft touch upon her face. Startled and confused but still she stood gazing into the mirror. With curiosity she touched her own face the same as she touched the mirror. This time she would feel the cold and smooth glass. Over and over she would test this paradox of reality. It took many times before an understanding would find a way into her thinking. With this understanding she acknowledged with a smile of crimson and ventured on. She found strength and wisdom that day with the lesson that how we see ourselves is the image we reflect.

The morning rain steps aside for the majesty of the afternoon sun. With just a glance from the sun every remnant of the morning rain glistens brightly in reflection. A reflection with more power than sight can fully endure. It is with this limited sight we achieve the trueness of the offered visions. Even as we squint or shade our eyes we can more clearly envision and imagine the spectacle that is our soul. It is as if the sun awaits the rainy days to offer us the gift without any expectation of response other than our growth. It remains a mystery why when our sight is full we miss the important things with life. The sun creates its own reflection by always shining brightly regardless of the storms that come and go. One could perceive the true message is to always shine brightly without any expectation and the unexpected reward will be found in the reflection around us.

Once again, a storm was bearing down upon them. With fear and forsakenness, they reacted, just as they had many times before. It was in hiding they would wait for it to pass by or through them. Those that would survive unscathed would lay claim to faith as the rest would relinquish any claim of faith. On one particular moment ahead of a pending storm one man stood against the crowd and decided to face the storm and no longer be controlled by the fear it represented. Not only did he stand facing the storm but walked toward it. The crowd would warn him of what would happen should he continue to openly face the storm. Without changing the focus of his eyes and soul he responded to the crowd one last time. "Unlike you I choose to walk with faith and not wait for it to be bestowed upon me." From hiding the crowd watched the storm consume him until he was no longer visible. They would never see him again and assumed that he had perished. It was a year later that a letter arrived addressed to THE CROWD. Since no one wanted to dare assume any responsibility for the crowd they gathered together and argued about who should open the letter. Finally, they handed the letter to a child to open. Once open they rushed freely to view the contents. With great surprise they found only a picture of a man. The man in the picture resembled the one who faced the storm and was thought gone forever. As they all had to see the picture they did eventually notice there was writing on the back. Free from any guilt now that the child had opened the letter on of the crowd read the letter aloud for all to hear. "You all were wrong. I faced the fear armed only with my faith and I survived. I no longer hide from life and have found it gloriously enlightening. I was changed forever by the storm but for the better. One must walk with faith, not hide from it." the envelope and the picture were left lying there on the ground until the next storm would carry it beyond their comprehension.

The picture paints a blue jean skirt, red high heels, with a crimson red smile. The image forever etched with regret and time merely adds vividness and clarity. Even though it is one of many such etchings it contributes proportionately to the library of regret. The purpose of the library is a place of reference and referral. Also in proportion is the volume of the library compared to achievable wisdom. None of the images no matter what they portray appear twice. The mistake we often make is in failing to recognize that learning is never a regrettable experience. Embrace your regrets as lessons and not definitions.

The deceptions of society would lead a naive traveler to board a ship promising treasure and fortune. He would leave behind everything unknowing of their later importance. He would set sail on this quest with great enthusiasm and commitment. Blinded and occupied by the diligence required to ensure a continued and successful journey he failed to notice the emptiness upon which he sailed. It was not until the shore was lost from sight that he would realize the feeling of being captive and merely instrumental to the quest of another's hopes and dreams. Many times, he would look beyond the ship to only see the vast and treacherous emptiness surrounding him. Fear of the unknown and the fear that he would surely fail and perish beyond the vessel that held him prisoner. Days would lead to years and then became a life of regret. More and more often the thoughts of abandon would swell within in him greater than any swell of compliance the sea upon which he sailed could offer. One morning as the sun would rise and he found himself alone and captain of the ship he sailed. With this inspirational moment he realized that he was truly the captain of his own ship. He allowed any regret to fall and sink to the depths of the sea. As he looked around to see no one he again looked into the orange glow of the sunrise he found warmth and a faith that was the treasure and fortune that he had long sought. It was in that moment that he would find himself standing at the edge of the ship he had long been a traveler. With his eyes closed from the brightness of the sun he leaned into the warmth and fell into the sea of life. He swims there still and forever with the mermaids of myth and faith for guidance.

Imagine the first traveler as he came upon the darkness where we now find light. With the soul of a gardener he would bring light and life to a garden of his creation. Eternally he tended to this garden of life and it grew vast and beautiful. One day as he looked out upon his garden he felt something was missing that would connect it all together. He decided his garden needed something of him as the creator. The miracle of children was already within his power but he wanted a son of his own. He could have just created a son but he believed another of his creations could not be improved upon. A life already within his garden would be to whom he trusted in the creation of his only son. He chose the one he felt could create a miracle beyond his ability. He freely gave up a part of himself to too one of his creations and witnessed a miracle within a miracle. With his son the garden became connected and one. Eternally he would be grateful and cherish the creation known merely as a mother. Shouldn't we also share the gratitude eternally and especially on a day we call Mother's Day. HAPPY MOTHERS DAY!!!

It was with great enthusiasm and excitement that he ran to the dock from which his dreams were soon to set sail. He anxiously waited for those, whom had committed, to join him. His crew did finally arrive to find him waiting. He would board the ship time and time again but his crew of merely one would not follow. Every day he could see the ship but it remained tied to the dock. After a time, the dream of sailing gave way to merely living on a vessel destined to sail the sea but existing anchored to the land. Even more time would find him living alone on a ship that would never sail. Day after day he would watch the rope give release but would always reach a point of impact that just drew him back as though he also was bound and a prisoner of a dream that would never venture beyond his own mind and thoughts. As the rope grew weak it would tease with ever growing but still limited freedom. From this existence of solitude his mind grew into a state of independence. Soon he would no longer feel the need for help or crew to navigate and sail this mighty ship upon the seas of his dreams. One day as he stood alone on deck watching the rope grow tighter as it approached that limit that would force return he ran and with a sense of anger and regret and cut the rope cleanly and completely. His heart was now beating through his chest with anticipation of freedom. The freedom he sought so dearly was now visualized as just being adrift and powerless. The ship did slowly drift away from the dock but again was a prisoner of another source. As he waited for distance to increase it became clear that he was just drifting back from whence he came. The frustration only gave energy to the anger and regret that he thought had set him free. Even if only to himself he felt he had said all the right words and found belief in all the right thoughts. As he came closer and closer with the tide back to the dock he knew to return at this pace would surely mean to crash. As he came close enough to see the rope from the dock floating upon the sea he relived the act of cutting the rope to gain his freedom. From this mental review a sense of clarity fell upon him. This time with an action filled with encouragement and faith he raised the sails of his ship. Breathless he looked up to the sails and with a thunderous crash his breath was restored as it was captured in the sails and instantly put him in control of the ship and his dreams. He turned the ship away from the dock and what lay before him drew his attention away from what was for so long behind him. Free to choose now where he would venture and forever grateful for the ever-changing breath that would fill his sails and allow this freedom and peace.

Words and thoughts alone are not enough to move you through your journey. You have to act in your own behalf just like turning the page to read the next chapter of the book of you.

Their existence shall be eternal even though they claim a lifetime. They linger like ghosts in search of closure. They remain always close enough for their thoughts to be always heard as whispers upon our soul. They are relentless and never need rest and even grow in strength within our silence. With outstretched arms of crowd control, we travel and grow weak from the constant fear that they will overtake us and obscure our vision. Many moments are missed along our journey as we look back to ensure they remain behind us. The crowd may and will surely grow as our journey gains length but none are ever truly set free. When we think we are alone it becomes clear that we are not and will never be. Always a whisper away they can become overwhelming and blur our perspective. It is not because of any action on their part but because of our own reaction to feeling pushed beyond our faith. It is not until we lose control and they surround us that we come to understand why they remain. They remain as examples, reminders, and protectors of our soul. Once they are no longer held captive they become part of the aura that surrounds us and carries us on our journey.

It is only with the release of control that we shall truly obtain it. Life's journey will develop more clarity and understanding as we go if we learn to listen to the ghosts of regret.

The moon was full but as it moved in and out of the dark clouds it was warning of a storm approaching. The port of the little town sat silent and empty but the people of the town knew he would soon arrive. They knew that on a night of a full moon painted with darkness he would visit their little town. The stories that were told of his ritual arrival were gossip among those who lacked the courage to even be witness to his presence. He would always arrive alone aboard the ship of darkness he sailed. Never was there ever a mention of a crew that was ever seen. He was thought to be a man but his many wounds lay open and from each one a fierce and blinding light would pierce the darkness. The light was so blinding that no one could look upon his true image. He made no effort to draw attention to his presence but all would notice him but from a safe distance. He would always just seek a place that he may rest and wait out the storm. No one dare getting close enough to even know the nature of his words if he even had any. They all knew that when the storm had passed he would again continue upon his journey. As he would leave there port the light that consumed him would fade as the sea swallowed him away and vanished as again the moon shined full and cloudless. On this particular night the stories would find their truth and forever change. A newcomer to the little town and the owner of the store on which he chose to seek rest and refuge, was awakened by his light as it shined through her windows and the cracks and crevices of her stores soul. She was aware of the stories and was afraid of this unknown. She did not attempt to open the door but just spoke through the door and asked the stranger what he wanted. She waited for what seemed an eternity with the fear racing through her. Finally, she heard a voice from the darkness. In a soft and gentle voice, he said "I mean you no harm and all I seek is shelter and a place to rest as I wait out the storm and then I will be on my way. If that is not acceptable I will find another place away from you." All the stories suddenly lost some credibility with his tone and manner of speaking. With his lighted wounds still burning through her door she felt her fear ease. She then responded and said "no, I have no issue with offering you my porch. How did you become so badly wounded and is there anything I can do to help you?" He replied, "I appreciate your kindness. I have been hurt many times and just can't seem to heal from within." Any fear that she may have had was now gone and forgotten. Again, she would speak and said "I want to open this door but I have to keep my eyes closed and won't be able to find my way so take my hand and lead me to you." She waited and when she still did not hear an answer she closed her eyes ever so tightly and threw open her door and stepped out onto the porch and waited. Within moments she felt the roughness and strength of what must have been his hand and he pulled her closer to him. She then pulled herself even closer and threw her arms around him and hugged him with all her might. He softly asked "what is it you are doing, I don't want to hurt you." As she continued to hug the strange sailor she replied to his question in a firm and assertive voice, "I intend to hug you so tightly that all of your wounds will have no choice to close and I intend to hold on until they heal from within you." He did night fight her intentions and remained within her embrace hoping and believing more and more as she maintained and consumed him within her embrace. Suddenly the full moon escaped from the dark clouds that held it prisoner and shined down seemingly with purpose upon this little town. As the towns people came out from hiding with this sign they cautiously proceeded to look for and found the absence of the stranger's light. One did notice his ship still at port and warned the town but he was not to be found. On the porch she felt the heat of his wounds no longer were shining with the intensity as when he arrived and she open her eyes to see his eyes looking into hers with gratitude and compassion. She sat with him and watched the town look for something or someone they had never had the courage to see.

The road was open before as well as behind me. The sun was shining even when it could not be seen. The clouds were the purist of white and appeared motionless. The air was of chill and only seemed to get colder the more you would push to pass thru it. Just when it would be perceived to be unbearable a rush of warm air would consume your body and soul. The warmth was just enough to change your perception from one of retreat to one of perseverance. The clouds that appeared motionless would look differently and changed every time you would look up to them. The chill of the air may even bring a state of numbness but it surrenders quickly to the warmth when it comes upon us. Life itself can mimic this perception with a tremendous regularity. Is it strange, or intended the lesson that can be repeated and reassured from a Saturday motorcycle ride.

It was like she knew something I didn't. It was like she saw things that I couldn't. It was like she believed in something I didn't understand. Life is truly a gift but a shared gift. As we may speak of our life as an individual gift the truth is that it is a gift we share with all things. Life does not exist because we claim ownership but it is we that exist because of life. From her actions I soon realized that it was not that I didn't understand but had merely forgotten the truths we are all born with. There is no my life or your life but merely just life as it exists in everything. We are all players, so to speak, on the same team. The little girl that walks through the woods and picks only one flower of many because she knows that one represents the same message as many. The little boy, that see's the true nature of a man's soul. A good life is one lived in harmony, not in resistance. Learn from our children and ask yourself what kind of team player you are. Peace.

The path we walk can often seem to have no direction. It is when we think we are lost that we seek that direction in all things. We happen across the tracks of a path and become intrigued by its straightness and seeming length. As we easily divert our energy and attention to walking the track all seems good. Slowly we begin and step by step we perceive progress. But as we walk just a short distance we realize the steps to be uncomfortable with regard to the rhythm of our mind and body. As we increase the pace we find we cannot maintain walking and stumble. As we stumble we stop and then start again only to find stumbling to be even more common as we focus so much on the tracks that we can no longer walk and see our destination at the same time. Some will continue to try and fall and some just stop and look back to where they came from and a fortunate few will realize that they were not meant to walk any other path but their own. Just because the track may appear the quickest and straightest way to get some where does not mean it will lead where you are meant to go. You can stumble and fall until you see others that you thought were behind you now passing by you. They pass by you as they walk tracks meant for them. A journey is not all about straight but can involve many twists and turns. As a wise man once said, "Keep your destination in your sights and if you run out of straight then turn and your destination will turn with you." Peace.

Somber tones take their turn in awakening us to a world of somber shades and perspectives. It is with the power like the moon they hold us. With seemingly no desire or will to move we remain to the point where any distinguishing characteristics blend away and disappear. The sound of a single voice echoes with strangeness against the consuming somberness. We don't recognize the voice at first and our focus is more on whom it would be speaking too rather than the words spoken. When we do by chance listen enough we realize the words are our own voice calling for us from beyond or perhaps within the void we find ourselves. Time does not exist as we think we know it here and a moment could represent and eternity or an eternity could pass in a moment. The voice we hear to be our own does not give any clue to where it calls us from or too. We again lose focus of our own words and struggle to decide how to best reach them. Frustration can consume us to the point we just give up listening for the source of our perceived freedom and stand silent. It is in this silence we finally hear the words clearly and realize that they were being spoken from within us. It is now that we look within ourselves and as we do we can almost hear the click of the puzzle piece as it falls into place. Our vision will now come clear and color vividly fills the space within us and beyond us. The tones now claim a magical clarity and inspiration. As we may all wonder into this realm of non-existence it is the truths we hold within us that lead to our escape and freedom!

Everything felt so familiar today as he walked the beach lost in his thoughts. The rising sun was a painting he had seen before. The sounds of the ocean breathing in and out were in perfect rhythm to every gift of breath received without even noticing. As he looked out upon the vastness of the sea he would only feel so small and insignificant. As he came closer to the edge of the reach of the tide with hope it would soon reach him. Lacking faith and fearing it never would he stepped out into the water as it reached out to him. He watched the ripple he created until it disappeared from sight and believed it lost. At that exact moment she emerged from the blueness beyond him. She was a beautiful and mesmerizing sight that he felt a familiarity with but quickly dismissed. Closer and closer she would swim toward him. Matching the rhythm of the tide she would disappear then emerge from the ocean again and each entrance was more magical than the last. He stood frozen in place as she came close enough for him to the ocean blue color swirling like the tide within her eyes. He wanted to speak but could not even move from the state of capture she had brought upon him. She raised her hand as if to hush and calm his effort and spoke to him in words that fell like music to his ears. "The ripple you create has summoned me many times and every time your wishes reflect a place of your past like the one you create now. I warn and remind you again today that to travel to the past means to leave any lessons or knowledge as they can only be carried forward. This circle you create for yourself will be never ending unless you acknowledge and embrace the faith to move on. I represent the gifts and miracles that lay ahead of you and each time we meet you choose that which is behind you. Again, I stand before you and offer you a wish to be granted and await your choice." Still frozen in the sands of time and unable to say the words of his choice he reflected upon her words. Maybe this was his choice every time or maybe he finally was able to continue forward were the thoughts consuming his mind. In a leap of faith, he found the strength to reach his hand toward her. With a smile that threw shadow upon the now risen sun, she reached out and took his outstretched hand into hers. She pulled him toward her and the wind gusted across the sea and consumed him and they both vanished into the blueness of her eyes perhaps to meet again or perhaps harmoniously forward.

The sun shines its brightest when in contrast to the dark clouds that appear ahead or behind it. The enhanced color and warmth are given as reassurance of continued perseverance. The clouds that the sun always fights thru but are given too much light behind can soon appear again ahead of us again and again. The more light we allow to shine behind us only diminishes what the sun is able to give the moon to finish off any dark clouds that may remain. Whether we choose to be led by the sun or the moon the message is the same. The message would be to focus your light forward and eliminate any dark clouds from behind us to reappear and steal away the energy of our progression along our journey. That's why the sun shines so bright because it knows the storm ahead is a challenge it can easily overcome and success breeds success with faith.

Time was as much lost as he was as he wandered this forest of denseness. The entrance appeared open and inviting but soon became dark and dense. Every step became a struggle and often thought of turning back but was so lost he didn't know which way back even was. He grew very tired and the scrapes, scratches, and bruises were stealing away any energy he might have left to continue. As he looked for a place to rest everywhere seemed uncomfortable and painful. The search for contentment brought him to the largest tree he had ever seen. It looked like a tree but in place of leaves were images. The images were of people, places, things, and everything in between. Its branches were large and seemed to stretch over the entire forest in which he was lost. As he looked upon the tree and noticed an image of someone he didn't know but he felt if he could get there then he could find contentment and rest. He began his climb of the huge tree and reached the image and the limb of the tree there was wide and long enough for him to lie down. Once he lay down he noticed another image above him but this time it was the image of a place he had never been. As he looked up at it he thought if he could get there it would be better. Again, he would make the climb and reach the image and though the limb was a bit smaller it still offered a good resting place but this time it was shaped in such a way that he was in a seated position. Now seated and relaxing he lay his head back and was about to close his eyes when again an image would draw his attention. This image was something he recognized and represented the reward he deserved for all his effort. Climb on he did until he reached this image but the limbs were so small and weak at this point that it offered no opportunity for healing. Now holding on with any and all the energy his soul could provide he looked out beyond the tree to see a lush, green meadow lit with the warmth of the sun. As he looked upon the meadow he realized he was within a very short distance from it when he began his climb of the tree of images. Now as he looked down he also realized he no longer had the energy or the courage to climb down. The branch on which he was clinging gave way and released him to will of the huge tree but it would not let him go and there he remains still. A wiser man would have searched for contentment within himself instead of wasting himself in the acquisition of those things outside him.

It was late in the day and I was killing time as I awaited the regenerating power of the sunset. I happened across a flea market and it looked abandoned by the crowds that had filled it earlier in the day. But that was a comforting draw for me and visited with no real visions of acquisition. As I wandered from table to booth throughout I came across a table with only a single item on display. I was intrigued by the concept of everything else that must have been there selling out. This last item was a small box that looked very old. I didn't see how it opened or even if it did. As I fumbled with it for a few seconds I was startled by the owner who seemed to just appear from nowhere. I laughed at myself for my surprised reaction as she asked if she could help me. I found it a little odd since I was looking at the only item on the table. I asked if the box opened and she said "yes it opens many things". She seemed to sense my confusion by her answer as she smiled but offer no other words. I then asked what was in it and she replied "whatever you want it to hold". Now I knew I was being played so I just asked what it was. She again smiled finding humor in her evasive answers to my questions and said it is a time machine. This time I laughed with disbelief and just waited for her to deliver the truth. She just stood there almost frowning at my disbelief and the way it must have shown upon my face. After we stood starring each other down for what seemed an eternity she was still silent but touch the box and it opened up into a strangely shaped mirror. As I looked closer she then asked me "where did you go?" I responded not with words but with a look of confusion. She then said "it is a time machine and you did not believe at first but as soon as I opened it for you to gaze into I could tell you found the ability to believe and that's why I asked you where you went in time. As I considered her words I realized she was speaking the truth. I was skeptical at first but when opened up to the possibility I did travel to a place in time that was dear to me. I asked her how much for the box and she again just stood there smiling at me. I again asked her how much she wanted for it. She replied "it is not for sale because once you have opened its possibilities you carry them with you always and have no need for it. I was disappointed and somewhat confused as to why it was displayed if it were not for sale. The sun was coming close to its glorious stage of setting and as I gazed upon it I found the truth behind what she had said. Outside I was lost in the sunset but within I was traveling to many destinations with the ease of just a thought. And with ease my soul was free.

His friends always meant well but they didn't always understand. One night they insisted that he get out of hiding and come to a party with them. He wanted to say no and part of him wanted to say yes. Finally, he did agree but the thought was scaring him to death. It had been a long time if ever that he had felt comfortable in that sort of environment. Of course, his friends would say "you never know you could meet the woman of your dreams", to which he would roll his eyes and them and dismiss the concept. The place was crowded when they arrived which just made the anxiety worse but he forced himself to engage. As he sat as alone as possible in a discreet corner trying to just blend in, his friends would not allow that for long. One of his friends rushed over and excitedly said "I don't about you but I just saw the woman of my dreams playing pool." Of course, I had to ask how he knew she was the woman of his dreams and all he could say was "look at her!" This is where they don't always understand. I too, dream of the perfect woman for me but not the same way my friend did. I was happy for him and I encouraged him to pursue his dream, so to speak. As my friend rushed away and left me alone in my safe corner I heard a voice from behind me. It was a woman's voice but I could not see her because she was sitting on the other side of the wall and I didn't dare get up and look stupid. Again, she spoke and asked me "don't you see the woman of your dreams anywhere?" as she laughed at the prospect. Of course, I said no, but it doesn't work quite like that for me. I quickly replied by asking if she saw the man of her dreams. She replied "no, not hardly". They spent the rest of the evening talking about topic after topic. His friend never did come back but he really didn't mind as he was enjoying the conversation. After a brief silence she asked if she could ask him a question which is not usually a good thing. But of course, he said sure. She then asked "what do you mean it doesn't quite work like that for you?" I was a bit bewildered at first but then I realized she was referring to finding the woman of my dreams. "I am not like my friend in that he dreams of a woman and sees her face and body and physical characteristics and thinks he has found her when he sees someone who matches that description. I also dream but I never see the things he does. The woman of my dreams appears to me as a soul and heart and speaks to me without having to be seen." He waited for her response but it never came. His friend finally showed up saying they needed to go. As he stood up he couldn't resist the temptation to look over the wall and see who he had been talking too. To his surprise there was no chair on the other side and there was no one even sitting close. His friend is pulling on his shirt at this point to go so he laughed to himself and just felt thankful for the conversation. He asked his friend where the woman of his dreams was and he said "didn't work out".

The climb was long and arduous to the top. The view was well worth the effort and sacrifice. The longer you choose to remain there at the end of your climb the more you begin to wonder why it no longer feels enough. Even at the top there are hills and valley's that continue to challenge you but the joy of accomplishment loses its luster and becomes unfulfilling. As you choose to remain and walk the paths of habit over and over again hoping for a reward you know will not come. You fear the loss of what you have even though you know it can never be taken away and will always be within you. You change and grow because of it and desire things differently than when you first began the climb. As you look out upon life from your current perspective you realize there are other mountains to climb that offer a new inspiration and motivation. The fear and regret involved in climbing back down this mountain to seek another is filled with risk and failure. It's with the realization that nothing can ever be taken away and to climb down would not be to move forward that we can see and sense a truth. It is a truth that teaches us that once we reach the top of one mountain we have learned what we need to know if we only allow it to guide us. We have to harness that faith that got us this far and learn to fly. Fly from the mountain that once encouraged you and seek another that will enlighten you. Leave behind that which no longer serves you and fly to much greater destinations just as our journey is meant to be.

The pale white crescent moon contrasted by an otherwise empty blue-sky page and underlined by the orange glow of the setting sun was the catalyst for inspiration in this moment. We cannot see the moon in its entirety but we know and imagine it whole. We cannot see the sun but we know it has already begun its journey of return. The empty blue sky can be perceived as a blank page awaiting our direction of creation. The events of the moment that led us upon this image fade quickly but we find gratification for the powers at work that bring us exactly where we need to be. Our perspectives cleansed and reborn of faith we find the energy, desire, and enthusiasm to continue on with purpose and priority. Our journey can be renewed in a moment if we only choose to accept it as it comes instead of expecting it to come as we direct. Open yourself and allow the magic to flow thru you as it flows through all things.

We can be drawn by a bright and visionary light to follow when its only power over us is that which we imagine and give it. We exude more energy contemplating that which we want to be and very little in the acceptance as things are. Freely we walk unprotected into the grasp of the reassuring glow of what may be. Soon we can find ourselves lost and vulnerable at the mercy of the darkest of storms. We remain within the storm driven by our imagined hopes. These hopes fade differently for everyone based on our conviction but when the time is right they do vanish, like the light that drew us out, into the darkness of the unknown and unaccepted. Whatever the length of time it takes we all search for that place to weather the storm. We will find or create this place of body, mind, or soul. It becomes an escape and a safe place for us to endure the harshness of the storm we find ourselves subjected to. As this escape provides us courage to be free from its grasp it also provides safeguards for our protection. One day we will venture beyond the storm and again be warmed by the hope and light offered there but not as brightly as before. The storm falls behind us as we move forward but the environment and characteristics of the escape remain strong and long with us. Forever changed for the better will come once we accept that we have the ability to protect ourselves no matter what storm we may encounter and set fear free. Otherwise we will spend eternity escaping the escapes we create.

The day seemed much longer than any other I had experienced as it seemed everything from my past was catching up to me. I hadn't noticed but the path I was walking was narrowing more and more as the day drug by. When I did notice, the light of the day was growing dimmer as darkness was approaching. I thought about turning back but behind me clouded in complete darkness. The narrowing path seemed to be leading to a single doorway just ahead of me. The closer I got I could see the door was just barely open but there was no light from where it led. Again, I looked behind, and was reminded of its complete darkness as it drew closer to me. I had to make a choice to turn back into the darkness, stand still and let the darkness overcome me, or step into the unknown darkness which lay ahead of me through the open doorway. As I pushed the door open further it still remained a vision of darkness. As I summoned what courage I could muster I stepped past the open door cautiously. In that instant a light overwhelmed and consumed me. I struggled to even see against its brightness. I was just there standing in a place so bright I could feel the heat through my closed eyes. I tried to back up from where I came but I could not find the door behind me. Again, I searched for courage as I shielded my eyes as best I could with my hands. The blurred vision I could see was what seemed to be many people surrounding me. After a few moments I gained the clarity to realize it was a place made of mirrors and every direction I looked I could only see my reflection, a reflection enhanced by the warmth and brightness of the light. I became unsure if it was the light that was preventing me from seeing clearly or the image of myself surrounding me. I was not happy with the images but after a while I did accept them and my eyes adjusted so I could see more clearly. As soon as I was able to accept the images fully I was also able to another partially open door ahead of me. I wasn't sure if it was that I had come thru to arrive at this place or the one that would lead me beyond it. I could see light beyond it but not as bright as where I was. The pace at which the darkness chased me here I could not imagine any light would show thru the door behind me. With faith I stepped thru the open door ahead of me.

His thoughts betrayed him as they teased him with the memory of her scent and touch but her physical presence remained denied. A presence so mesmerizing that the moment would surely pass before him as he remained silently questioning the reality of it. A moment that could be realized without even eyes to gaze upon as it has been so rehearsed that the heart would know long before the thoughts could seize any sort of control. Thoughts portrayed as a dream but held in check by the truth within the soul. A pointless search of sight awaiting the crossing of paths of two souls destined for one another but not destined to decide when, where, or how. The mind would transform dreams into faith and the heart would evolve them into trust. The thoughts would create such a familiarity prior to any chance encounter that they would immediately become as one. The idea that for every thought he would envision there was another finding the magic of it. And in that magic, find comfort that she was already part of him and he was part of her. As he goes forward strengthened by an unseen bond he has trust in his faith that the moment will be like the birth of a star and its light will travel on through eternity.

The day started as usual with inspiration from the rising sun. Its glory soaked in for a few moments giving the serenity to carry on with awe and appreciation. This day the sun's warmth was strong and persistent. The pavement was hot and dry but teased with the image of cooling moisture always just ahead. To walk the pavement on such a day is usually done so expeditiously and silently. This day however the silence is disturbed and curiosity slowed the pace. The sound of rushing water could be heard from below the manmade pavement of protection. Storm drains by definition, but a window of life by perception. Thoughts of water running lead us to imagine the blood that flows through our veins unseen and unheard but vital to our existence. When we contemplate life we quickly refer to ourselves but the truth is that we are only a part of it. What other signs do we dismiss because we are unwilling or unable to see, hear, or even feel them? Imagine the sound the flower makes as it blooms or how a weed must feel growing through the barriers we construct as it stretches upward toward the sun. We spend our days thinking life exists because of us but we merely exist as one of the many miracles of life. The struggles and challenges we create pale greatly in comparison to the gift all things share. Allow the signs to flow through you like water flows beneath our feet and freely allow the enlightenment of life to carry and consume you.

It was in a moment of silence and reflection created by the many challenges and disappointments in our busy life. You look out upon the vastness of the parking lots and buildings they are built around and you quickly realize you are one of many processing tasks one priority after another. A glimpse of green catches your eye because it exists where it should not. It existence is testament that we can never truly hide the nature of the life we share. You look even further in the distance and on a hill overlooking everything is a house.

It is a very old house that was surely built to be a home. You can imagine the view from this house and wonder if those who first stood there and found it worthy of a home had any idea what the view would become over time. I can imagine standing there admiring the beauty and deciding that this would be the perfect place. Then I wonder when we no longer need automobiles to travel, what will become of all the masks we no longer need? The smallest weed that looked out of place predicts that nature will reclaim that part of itself long lost. I can hear with such clarity the words of the future as it once again looks out and says "this is perfect"!

The road is never clear and many times you will fall to the ground. As you lay there in a state of disorientation all you can see is the blueness from above giving no clues or insight. You rise to your feet once again and in the stillness, you search for your direction. Moments along the way are few and far between due to the pace at which you have traveled focused only on the destination. Every direction you consider share's the same sense of doubt and fear as the other. Once you choose a direction you will encounter the vague sense of familiarity but with no assurance. In time you believe the familiarity to be created in your mind as a wish or hope. You continue on and regain that same pace that will lead you to your next fall. Again, and again we fall until we realize that it is the moments along the way that are our compass and the destination pales in comparison to what the journey has to offer. It is along our journey that we collect the moments that become our wings when we reach the next phase of an endless journey. Our destination is defined by each and every moment we allow to change us along the path of infinite spiritual evolution.

I could taste her name upon my lips but could not speak it. The sound of her voice echoed within my soul but I could not hear it. Her appearance walked the hallways of my mind like a ghost but I could not see her. Her thoughts merged with mine but I could not distinguish between them. With every sunrise I feel the warmth of her heart and with every sunset I see the colors of her soul. Within every wind that blows I feel her breath upon my skin. I face the rain so I can taste her tears of joy and sadness. I seek the beauty within devastation because I know she is there waiting. She waits for me as I wait for her and become even more deeply connected as every moment passes. It is with faith and trust we wait, knowing that the moment we meet and become whole will be the moment that defines us. From this defining moment we will continue on hand in hand as one soul on the eternal journey of enlightenment.

The ad offered room and board in trade for work around the home. He answered the add with interest and the woman he talked to told him she would consider what he had to offer and let him know. That night was the most restless sleep he had ever experienced. It was like something was stirring about in his mind all night looking for something. The next morning the call came early as she accepted him for the position she advertised. The day he arrived to the run-down farm house and went to the door he found a note pinned to the door welcoming him and giving instructions. He let himself in and made himself at home and then reviewed the list of tasks he was to complete. When he came down stairs he noticed a plate of lunch was left and attached was another note. The note was on the same old and yellowed paper that the one at the front door. The note was a reminder of the tasks that were needed done that day. Every day he would find a plate for breakfast, lunch, and dinner left for him with another note but he never saw her. It was only at night as he slept that he heard the ring of china and the creaks from the stairs and hallways within the house that he was reminded of her presence. The days led to weeks and then to months and he had never seen her but he knew she was there. One day as he was at the lumber store picking up supplies that she had left the money to buy the clerk asked him where he was working. He told the older man behind the counter about the ad he answered and where he was working. The clerk just stood there with a look of confusion and silent. He asked the clerk if something was wrong and the clerk said "I know the house you speak of and I knew the woman who lived there but she died about twenty years ago." He looked at the clerk and told him that he must be thinking of a different house. All the way back he couldn't get the clerks words out of his head and then he thought about the fact that he had never seen the woman he was working for. With a little chuckle within himself he just accepted the possibility. As he returned to the farm house with his supplies it was time for lunch. As he went to accept his usual plate and note he was surprised by a heartfelt hello upon his ears. She was there awaiting his return and as she looked into his eyes a truth was shared between them. In the softest of voices, she said "this is my home and it always will be." He asked her why he had never seen her before now and she smiled and said "because you did not believe in the possibilities until now."

I find that the choices in life can be as subtle as the direction we might focus our eyes. In one direction are the grayish blue clouds of a pending storm. They paint the sky so fully and completely that they make seeing easy and effortless. In another direction is the setting sun resting just at the tops of the trees in the distance. The sky is mixed with an openness and clouds of many shapes and colors. The sun shines with a light so piercing that it is difficult to maintain sight without almost closing your eyes and maintaining the vision within your mind. In this moment I chose the sun even with the struggle involved. As I squint and admired the majesty of suns power I heard the rain coming from behind me. I resisted the urge to turn away and stayed focused on the light. Soon the rain was falling upon me and my sight became eased with the filtering of the rain across the vision of the setting sun ablaze. Now as I looked into the sun I was looking thru each drop of rain and within each and every one was the colors of a rainbow. In that moment I was part of the rainbow powered by a setting sun. Now every time I see a rainbow I will remember being a part of it and in that I find the faith and belief to seek miracles even within those places that are hard to see.

The sound of drums in the distance softly beckoned for attention. As their desire to be recognized grew stronger so did their intensity. Brandishing a sword of light to further announce its coming it would strike vigilantly against the beautiful blue contrasted sky. Everything green would bow in recognition of its approach. The roar of a waterfall drew closer and closer until everything became consumed by its cool and cleansing touch. Many lonely souls now in its embrace find enlightenment in its magic of bringing shape and visibility to those things unseen or forgotten. All on parallel paths the many parts of a soul can now see on another and once again become whole. An older man will find the child within him for courage and curiosity and the child will find the older man for wisdom and encouragement. From this encounter a renewed passion and faith in the journey will be born from the simplest of things such as a thunder storm.

The lonely nights evolved over time into a state of numbness and denial. The windows of the soul covered in the attempt to control the light that might enter but in turn throwing shadow upon the light within. The goal may well be to be unnoticed but it is the dimness that becomes more obvious when exposed to light. The soul's windows hint at light but just at the edges and just enough to gain that which was hoped to be avoided. The souls true path to peace is allowing itself to become consumed by the light and use the energy to shine brightly even within the darkness. Our true path can only be seen when illuminated by the light that burns within us from faith.

The standoff with fear was slowly stealing away any strength left within me. The steps backward had brought me to a place I perceived no return. I could feel the edge cutting into my heels as I continued to stare into the darkness. That which lay behind me was so be consumed by the darkness of the known and familiar past but that which lay ahead was unknown and unfamiliar. It was clear if I turned the direction the fear pursued was to be forever imprisoned by it. To go forward was filled with risk of failure and a responsibility to react to success if achieved. It came down to deciding upon one of two choices. Settling for the comfort of those things behind me or having faith in a future ahead of me. The longer I remained at this edge the more I could feel the blood leaving the vessel of my body as my soul frantically beckoned my mind to listen before it was too late. The run forward seemed longer than I remembered stepping back but I continued on. Every stride forward I could feel the momentum growing and when I could no longer resist I dove into the darkness with the faith of a knight. It was a violent entry but quickly turned to silence as I descended into the darkness. When I had reached the limit of momentum I was floating in a black sea of weightlessness. As I let go of any control I felt the pull of an invisible force upon me. In the darkness and the silence, I was shifted to position that allowed me to see the greatest light above. It was not a bright and focused light but it was soft, warm, and consuming. It appeared to be coming closer to me but then I realized that I was moving closer to it. The closer I came the greater the sense of hope came over me. Unsatisfied with the pace and a growing desire to reach the source of the light I fought to reach it. Again, with a violent transition I sprang out of the darkness and a breath filled my vessel with life. My heart and soul pulled me into the rescue boat of faith as the both shook their heads saying "We told you so! You have to look up if you want to see the light."

It was their seventeenth summer and it would a time of the greatest joy and profound sadness. It would be the ending of one chapter and the beginning of another. It was a time when moments came and went without any expectation and were free to blossom unguarded. They say you can't truly know someone in the short time of a summer but the soul does not follow these rules. As soon as their eyes met their souls felt everything they needed to know if they were listening. Hand in hand they shared a bond that would forever change them. Time just seemed to stand still as they shared it together. The sound of their laughter would drown out any other sounds as they became lost in one another. The days passed and claimed the entire summer as a moment.

The time had come for them to return to the lives they had stepped away from if only for a moment. The sadness was a confusing emotion as each wondered and searched for a definition. Was it loss or was it love? She was first to have to go and you could almost hear the tear as they finally separated from the perfect hug. He watched her walk away until she was out of sight. Her walk was slow because she could not resist turning once again to gaze into his eyes. He was left on the beach alone but knew he also must leave soon. He sat at the edge of the oceans touch feeling each and every tear he cried drop into the salty water and disappear giving way to the man within him. There was no doubt how each of them felt about each other and it was a feeling they would never forget. He reached down and drew her name in the sand and said, to himself, when her name disappears I will go my way. The water would rush in and out over her name but it remained. It was society that beckoned him away but as he kept looking back her name remained. It was many years later that the boy now a man returned to place of his seventeenth summer. The first thing he did was to return to the beach where she existed so clearly and went to the water's edge where he had written her name. A passerby noticed his search and asked him if he lost something. He told her no, I was just looking for someone. She then asked him “who are you looking for?” it was at that moment that he saw it and brought his hands to his eyes in disbelief. Her name was still there written in the sand. The woman again asked “who?” As he stood up he turned to the woman and with the voice of his soul he said “faith”. As he looked into the woman’s eyes to gage her reaction she was smiling the smile of her soul. He could not look away and she every so softly spoke from her soul and said “I am faith and I am always with you”.

With tiny bare feet we walk into this mortal life. The light shines ever do brightly with hope and possibilities. The game of hide and seek offers the exploration with eyes open to the miracles around us. Time spent wandering the same hallways casts the shade of comfort upon the light. Tirelessly we walk the hallways hoping for more but only find what we are used to finding. The hallways are surrounded by walls we cannot see beyond and doors are hidden from view. The time we spend in this circle of comfort and familiar is different for each of us. It is not until we challenge all that is familiar and look away from the focus that consumes us in search of more. It is not until we look away from what lay behind as it continues to appear again in front of us. It is when we once again can look into the light with faith that the hallways of familiar will melt away and open up into a lush green meadow of hope and opportunity. So, when the shadows and shade of life lead us into darkness we have only to remember to look up to restore the purity and miracle that is life.

I have walked past this tree for over ten years and never truly noticed it until today. And even today I didn't notice it because it drew my attention. It is so fully consumed by other living green that you can't even see the tree that exists within. It is surely large enough to deny anything to exist so close but it does not. The green that encompasses it is so green that you have to touch it to see the extent of vividness. Without seeing the tree within, I can imagine its strength and confidence. It does not need to stand alone and it does not need to be seen. Without even being seen its character and soul are a vision of clarity that others challenge space in search of. Its true image is defined by the strength of life that surrounds it. The message I perceive from this moment of recognition is that we should seek to be seen by the beauty and strength we encourage, support, and inspire around us.

He found himself caught up in the storm of storms. He treaded the water of the turbulent seas as best he could, not being able or willing to swim. Many ups and downs confronted him before he soon gave in to will of storm. Upon awakening he found himself alone and forgotten on an island shark infested waters. He sat looking longingly out across the sea of doubt and disbelief. Out of nowhere came a ship surely to save him from his tragedy. The ship with the name AMRAK was too big to get close to the island so he would have to go to it. Reality raised its head as he could not swim and the waters around the island were shark infested. From the shore he cast a stone upon the sea hoping to judge the depth of the water. To his surprise the stone did not sink into the water. He cast another and it also just lay on top of the water like a stepping stone. He stepped onto the first stone and discovered it would hold him above the water. Stone after stone he cast and step by step he may his way to AMRAK, the ship of his rescue. He cast his last stone and realized he was not close enough to secure rescue and as he looked back all the stones had vanished into the sea. He could not and dare not swim for he would surely perish. The ship slowly started to move away leaving him standing on his last stone in the sea's unforgiving waters. At last resort he looked up to the sky and asked "why!!!!"? As he watched AMRAK disappear from sight he heard a soft voice upon the wind. "Had you not cast so many stones at others, you would have had enough to save yourself."

The river was a vision of stillness and silence. The characteristic of flowing water seemed hidden as the penetrating light of the evening sun was enhanced in the mirrored reflection. From the silence a boat appeared upon the river traveling in a mirrored stillness. It seemed to just glide across the top of the water without disturbance. Gently it passed and was soon gone from sight. In its path it left a void as if calling upon it to return. The water began lapping at the sides beyond its own limits as if to cry for the loss of the passer by. It slowly filled the void but then appeared as mirror broken into endless pieces. Each piece was now reflecting the evening sun in a display that could only be described as appreciation and jubilation. The pieces of glass danced with color through the setting of the sun and continued on with the emergence of the moon. The flowing river would seem forever changed but it was from within it would find the greatness and glory it possessed. Change that which lies within and it will be reflected joyously outward.

When he opened his eyes, he found himself at a shoreline tired and short of breath. It was a dark day but he brushed the clouds aside to expose the suns power to heal and reveal. As he turned away from the noise that led him here he found silence. With the help of the light he noticed a ship standing tall in the distance. The gentle breeze was soothing to his strained sight and with every surge seemed to be calling his name out of the silence. He walked across the water to the ship and with every step it became even more vividly defined. He went aboard the seeming empty ship with caution, curiosity, and desire. The dark and lifeless ship instantly rose up in the water in recognition of his long-awaited presence. Every step would be painted of returning color and life. As he touched the wheel the sails rose into tight attention as if awaiting his desire and direction. He looked out upon the openness and wonder of the sea as it sparkled under the sun and the wind would adjust the ship beneath him as if ready to carry him any direction he might beckon it. The shoreline was no longer visible and all that existed was he upon a sparkling blue sea of imagination and adventure. He settled his glance in the direction of the sun and the ship rose out of the water and sailed upon the wind as he flew toward the sun free at last. Even now as you hear the howl of the wind you know it is he aboard the ship named freedom with only his soul to guide him. What you can believe so can you achieve.

Each breath we take flows in rhythm to the ocean tide as it sweeps in and out. The emotions that guide us seem a reflection of the clouds as they journey across the sky from storms of sadness to breaks of happiness. We find nourishment from the sun and glow like the moon. As water promotes life on the planet, so does it promote life within each of us. All things share the same stardust as it was showered with purpose upon creation. Life is a spiritual collective of souls sharing the journey of growth until we are called upon to bring our unique color to the rainbow of light. What color will you bring?

The wind whistled its secret tune past the open window. Every time it sings it draws our attention and we look knowing we won't see it and truly never expect to see it. Again, and again it beckons and we comply with sensual recognition. We hear its song, we feel it's cooling touch, but we only see its effect. We see the trees dance to its song, the water ripple and rise beyond itself, seemingly lifeless dust and debris takes flight in celebration of its presence. Is its mysterious song one of faith? Sitting in a parked vehicle lost in time and space, awaiting a sign. The motor is running for fear it will not start again but it is not forward we fear losing but it is backward to the place we find security and courage to venture forward in our journey. As the wind whistles it offers the mind the vision to see what faith can do. All the forces are conspiring to bring encouragement and empowerment. When faith whistles will you see?

She knocked on the door but there was no answer. As she looked through the window of the door to see if anyone was home the door just fell open. It startled her but as she regained he composure she felt comfort in the fact that she was the only witness as there didn't appear to be anyone home. It was warm and felt strangely familiar. The lighting was dim but the light from the windows more than made up for it. She explored room after room and found no one but the familiarity grew stronger. If she was to ever have a home of her own she imagined it to look exactly like this. She shielded her eyes from the light that was pushing deep into the room as she looked out the kitchen window. The sun was sparkling across and crystal-clear lake surrounded by trees as if to hide and protect it. On the lake she saw a small boat just drifting with a woman. The woman looked to be about her age and the familiarity gained a strength that seemed to clench her heart. She stepped out the door to find herself standing in a lush green lawn that went to the edge of the gleaming lake and the little dock. She raised her hand in hopes of gaining the woman's attention as she drifted carelessly and seemingly content. The clinching of her heart insisted upon action so she began to speak aloud "hello" over and over and louder and louder she sought recognition. When it seemed, she was almost screaming the woman rose up from her position of contentment and happiness and their eyes met, just as the sun moved into a position that brought them both into a magical glow of clarity. She felt a pull on her shoulder that was taking her farther and farther away until she heard a voice ask "are you ok honey? You must have fallen asleep on the park bench and you seemed to be having a dream and you just kept screaming hello. Are you alright?" after the shock of being awakened eased she just smiled and said "yes, I am fine. I was dreaming of searching for something and I found it. It was within me the whole time but now I see. Thank you."

Day after day I watched the river run lower and lower. Subtly it ran dry and barren. It appeared to the eye as a scar upon the skin. A reminder of pain inflicted upon a prior glory. It was a glimpse of a lost dream. Nature was there to reclaim it into the collective but it would never be same. Rains would do their best to revive the life of the river but it was not enough. It would seem the scar of a river had given up hope. One cloudy day it grew very dark and the rain bellowed with strength and duration intent on proving its superiority. A dam that was built up stream on the river buckled under the cleansing torrents and again released the river to flow freely. The river now ran stronger and fuller than it ever had before. The dry river may have abandoned hope but nature's faith and commitment would not be denied. We all travel a unique river of life but when we allow it to be dammed up, it will be faith that brings freedom once again, more powerful and wise than ever before. It is a faith that will bring us past the barrenness we experience on our spiritual journey on the river of life.

The music from above begged my attention as well as my glance. The glance brought the robust and towering tree into focus. The tree led to a whimsical movement from within it. The movement came clear as two squirrels struggled to see which was happiest. The squirrels led to the flowers across the lush green yard. The flowers led to the explosion of two birds mimicking the squirrel's actions. The birds took flight and the melody followed them upon the wind. The wind was gently carrying the feel and emotion of the melody to all who would receive it. The world conspires to bring the miracles of healing and encouragement through us but we must choose to receive it. As we find the faith and trust to receive, so shall we find it in our ability to give.

Generally compliant to the expectations of normal the days pass. Normal can be that which is defined, as usual and typical behavior. It is within this passing time that we fail to acknowledge or understand the signs. The signs do show and reflect the message that to define something is not to control it. The search for definition serves only to place limits and boundaries. The winter snow falls pure and white over the land and is considered normal and defined as just winter in January. The winter sky can open up without notice and produce a day with a temperature of sixty plus degrees. The day is bright as it reflects from the winter snow as it awaits the opportunity to evolve. The snow is born in a state that allows it to evolve quickly. The snow that is altered or changed from its original state finds itself struggling to evolve and continue on its journey. The edges of roads turn dark and rough. The piles made from moving can remain long after this opportunity to evolve has passed. It would seem to show us that the more tightly we confine who and what we are the harder it becomes for us to evolve and continue the journey of life. It would also seem that those who choose to live by definitions of normal limit their opportunities to grow and evolve in the cycle of life. We should never define ourselves or anything we encounter. We should find happiness in being who we are and who we will become. In this part of our journey; the true path of enlightenment comes from reflection and release and not from definition and resistance. Open your eyes and unlock the world.

Two little girls were playing in the park under the very watchful eye of their mother. On a bench not too far away but seemingly alone and distant was an older man. At times he appeared to be very attentive to the surroundings as the children played and then he seemed to be lost in a dream. In those lost moments he was looking up into the sky and his arms lay wide open on the back of the bench. He looked like he was lost in a dream. The ball the children were playing with got beyond them and rolled directly toward the bench where the man was sitting. It was a strange roll in that it seemed to have a mind of its own. The children just stood there in amazement as it came to rest at the man's feet. He was still looking up with his eyes closed and couldn't even had known it was there. The children looked at their mother for her support and reassurance and cautiously and quietly walked to the bench to retrieve the ball. Within in a few steps of reaching it the man slowly sat up and reached to pick up the ball as if he had known it was there the whole time. He smiled at the children and held out the ball for them. They thanked him and then could not resist to ask him what he was looking at up in the sky. He responded by saying "I was dreaming the dream you call life. I was listening and directing everything around you as you played and I could see your curiosity about me so I led you to me. My dreams are of your journey through yours." The children didn't really understand what he was saying but were glad he was nice as they trusted he would be. In this dream we call life it is our relationship with the true dreamer that paints the magical path of our journey.

The sun rises upon a lush green valley filled with magical colors and sounds that come so easily with youth. The questioning of curiosity leads us many times in exploration to where the old wooden fence stood to protect us from what lay within. The fence was made of worn and tattered wooden posts and splintered and weathered slats. The view inside the unknown fenced world looked similar to the one of comfort and safety we called home. We walk the fence line in search of the easy place to cross but we never find one. The rainbow of temptation begins at our feet but lands across the line into the land of unknown. Cautiously and carefully we climb over the fence in search of the unknown. Within a few steps we hear a sound or perceive an image that our minds translate as danger and we quickly retreat. In our haste we usually experience pain from the splintered wood as we clumsily climb back to where we know calm. Eventually we resort to crawling under because of the fear of pain and suffering experienced in a past failure. The same experiences that we remember painfully teach us lessons that help us stay longer and go farther across the fence. In time as we follow the rainbow of temptation and promise beyond the land of our comfort we realize the truth in such a glorious moment of clarity. The fence that all this time we believed existed to protect us from what lay beyond was really the image of our conditioned mind keeping us within its grasp. The key is that once we chase the rainbow across the fence to never look back to the fence and it will disappear forever as we travel freely beyond the boundaries of the conditioned mind and we will find the world open to our imagination through faith.

The tree of life will more generously yield fruit when the soul, mind, and body see the same reflection in the water of the river that feeds it.

"I WILL!" he exclaimed in such a deep and rumbling voice that it sounded like thunder. He the just simply turned and walked into the crowd until he was lost as one of them. From the crowd came the words "I know!" as the color red filled the evening sky as if to warn of the ending day and a reminder of appreciation for it. "I AM!" he proclaimed as he led the crowd toward a rising sun of new beginnings. As he became separated from the crowd of friends and foe the softness of his words was carried upon the wind with "I

MUST". From a state of pain and suffering he looked upon the crowd and said "THEY ARE!" now from high above the crowd he looked even higher and fought to whisper the word "WHY?" as the sky turned dark as if mourning. No longer would his voice be necessary to speak to the crowd as now his voice existed within the crowd and all he ever asked for was for a little faith as he exemplified. Search within and find yours.

The sun was still the master of the sky but it was sinking low upon the horizon. The lower it falls the bigger it seems. It was a smoldering hot day that seemed to grow even more literally breathtaking. It was a day away from work but it cannot be dismissed from all consciousness in such a short span of time. The day is spent mostly on the list of meaningful but yet meaningless tasks required in support of the fortunate opportunities which allow the day off. It seems like a merry go round without a conductor. The sun casts a golden haze as it filters through the blinds into the room in which I take refuge. The soft glow of the desk lamp is warm and comforting. I watch and listen as feeling guilty for not be involved in another activity and regret of feeling it necessary to submit to society expectations fight back and forth in my mind and knowing that fights never produce any winners. The fight is as much of a distraction in confrontation as each point is independently. I share my thoughts with you now as testament to the choice I made. Even as the sun filters through the window it shines upon me. The glow of the desk lamp surrounds me. The darkness between isolates and comforts me. As I express these words, the feelings that created them fall away and leave me room for new and better things. I choose to be my own conductor on the merry go round of life. Will you? Peace.

She was the vision of happiness as she ran across the field of flowers. So many glorious colors and yet not even one repeated. Her arms were extended to her sides as if she was leaping into the sky of dreams and fly. The petals of the flowers tickled her palms as she passed through them. With free will she ran her own course of creativity and desire. The farther she ran the less she could feel the flowers touching her soul through her palms. The vision was still compelling but the thought of losing touch became a distraction as she searched her soul for the reason of abandonment. Her now clouded mind diminished her capacity to see the true beauty as it was intended. She became lost in the cloud and stood still and wondered why? It wasn't until she looked continuously down she noticed the single flower dancing in the breeze at her feet. As she reached down to touch the flower she realized that all hope lay within her. She also realized that over time we can lose touch with those things that nurture our soul. With renewed spirit she began to run again and reaching down to the flowers she again came alive and her soul could fly again. What comes easy in youth must be reached for as we journey beyond innocence. Peace.

It was a day of struggle and self- manifested frustration. He could not wait for it to end and when he finally found silence of sleep the harshness of reality blended with the powers of dreams. He was awakened by the unbearable heat and weight of what consumed him. He opened his eyes but all was dark. He fought to free himself from the weight that held him and did gain some relief from the heat that must have destroyed all things by the smell of ash so overwhelming he could also taste the bitterness of it. He searched the darkness for even the hint of light and possibility and found it but it seemed far from his reach. With each step the unknown whispered of risk. No matter how much closer he came to the light it remained illuminated with the same degree of intensity as when he first discovered it. His hands outstretched in the darkness until finally he felt the light under his hand and sensing his touch the entire world burst into light. A light so bright that it hurt his eyes to look upon it at first but it quickly eased as if it knew his discomfort. From somewhere beyond the light he heard a voice say “we have power”. As he cooled his face in the now running fan and reached for a cigarette he thought to himself “do dreams control reality or does reality control dreams?” Peace.

I was sitting at the edge of lake, frozen so purely white that it glistened just to protect its existence. The bench on which I sat was weathered comfortably by the union of time and nature. I was watching and relishing in the setting sun, now the most glorious shade of crimson. Suddenly I became aware of what felt be the most beautiful woman my eyes have ever had the privilege to understand. She didn’t acknowledge my presence as she walked by or through me but as she softly stepped onto the frozen white lake she turned slightly toward me and gave the hint of a soft smile but quickly turned back. Her long flowing hair and dress was the same color as the setting sun and she was only visible with any distinction by the contrast of her vision against the frozen white lake. Step by step with bare feet she walked toward the setting sun and showed no sign of fear or doubt. She walked until the contrast vanished and she and the sun became one and suddenly both dropped from sight into the lake. In the same instant that she vanished beneath the ice the sun teased of rising behind me and the season had changed from winter to summer. I could not look away from the lake out of fear, or perhaps longing. Focused in the distance I was startled as the water splashed just in front of me. She rose from the depths of the deep blue lake. Her dress and hair now drenched and even a darker shade of crimson as before. Her drenched clothing allowed no secrets and her eyes could tell no lies. Again, she would glance slightly my direction and pose the most genuine and comforting smile accentuated by the fullness and softness of her lips of crimson. She gently walked toward the rising orange sun and into a breeze seemingly of her own creation. As she walked her hair and dress began to flow once again under the power of the breeze and the warmth of the rising sun. The frozen whiteness had been changed into the darkest shades of green and provided the contrast as she moved closer to the now crimson sun as it shined through her to meet my eyes. The contrast grew smaller and smaller until in an instant she vanished and all things turned dark as if expressing sadness with her loss. I now noticed the moon shining over my shoulder and I quickly turned in anticipation I found it full and the purest white with no contrast between it and the frozen lake other than the black star filled sky. I sat back on the bench with a sense of regret that I'm sure you will share in that I just sat there! Engage your dreams as reality and our reality will become that of dreams.

She found herself staring blindly upon the reflection of stone. Her mind wondered what it must be like to be cast away, alone, within a shell of stone. Her words had no effect upon the image as she imagined or hoped they could. The passing of time itself did nothing to soften the stone exterior. It wasn't until another would dare look upon the image that she realized that it was in her own reflection she sought change. He looked upon her reflection and also wondered its source and reasoning. His heart drew his hand and placed it upon the image of stone with kindness, concern, and compassion. As his warm hand touched her, a single tear came from within the eyes and rolled gently, dissolving the stone as it went. Again, he reached out and touched from his heart and another tear tore its way through the stone prison. He then reached out and embraced the entirety of her against and within him. With faith he held on as he felt the rigidness of stone give way to the warmth and softness that was her true image. When free she looked up and into his eyes to see that true reflection that she had longed for. He stepped back and set her free and his heart was strengthened more by the selfless gift than any he had ever received. Miracles come from within us as we travel the circle of life.

The struggles we encounter within this perceived reality are actually illusions of the conditioned mind. This perceived reality is consumed by the search for those things that offer brief and limited release from the illusions. We are always searching for happiness, pleasure, and even love. It is in these moments that we begin to feel the power and freedom but release them all too quickly so we may return to what we are conditioned to believe is reality. I propose that our true reality and perhaps destiny lie in the conditions and emotions that we spend this illusion looking for. Joy, happiness, pleasure, and love are found within us and it seems such a tragedy that we need or require catalysts to see and feel what we carry within our souls for eternity. Perhaps we should consider reality to be defined by those things we will take with us beyond this mortal existence as we continue the gift of our journey.

It is in the grayness of days that we learn to see the light in things we had yet to realize so when again the day turns bright we can close our eyes and feel the light around us.

Words bring us to the brink of a discovery that only the mind can explore. Peace.

Miracles are visible in the average as well as the extraordinary if we look for them instead of waiting for them to show us.

The more you argue with yourself the more familiar with the judge you become.

She chose the lake today inspired to venture beyond her comfort zone. It wasn't even visible to her conscience thought but the picture her sub conscience painted drew her to it. She began to doubt and feared a mistake as she pushed through the damp green forest that lay before as if to protect and obscure the secret. As she ducked under that last pine limb she stood before the contrasting openness of the lake she sought out. The water looked the shade of green as if a reflection of the boundary she had just conquered. There was a small and primitive dock the blended from the tall green grass into the equally painted water. A small canoe sat silent in the stillness of the water. Upon he knees she reached into the water as if to test for the truth of the color and the water ran crystal clear through her fingers. Reassured she looked up to sky and the sun met her with comforting warmth upon her face. The canoe was secured to the makeshift dock with a thin and tattered rope but it feels limp into the water as the canoe gave no resistance to where it waited. She looked around and found no one to see and felt inspired by coming this far alone. Gently and ever so cautiously she stepped into the canoe and sat down within it after moving the single oar that lay on the seat. She reached on the dock and pulled her backpack toward her, until she could lift it into the canoe without shifting the canoe. With ease she removed the little rope and set herself free, but remained motionless upon the water. She looked down to the oar and then back to dock. She gripped the dock and gently guided the canoe out onto the vastness of the lake. As the canoe moved like the sharpest knife, I sliced slowly through the still and silent water. The immediate sense of fear was strong as she drifted further away from the security of the dock. That initial fear soon faded away as she faced it head on. She then took the single paddle from beneath her feet and began to slowly drag it through the water and immediately felt her power to control her direction. From one side to another she paddled until the little dock was practically out of sight. It was her that she stopped paddling and let the canoe roam freely. She leaned back and dangled her arms over the side just so her fingertips were drifting with the canoe across the water. The sun was still bright and urged her to close her eyes and give in to the power of the moment. She could now hear the sounds of everything around her as she became part of everything. To be alone was her constant fear but in this moment, she realized she would never be truly alone as we all are part of everything and everything is part of us. She remained and felt the setting sun come and go. The moon rose so full and glorious and the next thing she knew she heard the gentle tap of the canoe to wood. The moon had brought her back safely to the little dock. She retied the little rope and climbed out of the canoe a different person. She still visits often to remind herself that to be by herself with faith, was to never be alone.

Each of us has their own unique and individual path to travel along life's journey. We cannot see another's any more than they can see our own. We might walk a path parallel to another for a day or maybe for eternity. We cannot follow another's path without risking the loss of our own if the once parallel paths drift in different directions. If we lose our road we will circle endlessly until we once again find it. To offer forgiveness is without substance and to forget goes against the core nature of the journey, which is to learn. There is no right or wrong to discover and declare. There is only knowledge and appreciation for what was truly shared instead of regret and bitterness for the perceived loss. It is with faith that we paint with all the glorious colors of our true essence.

To be missed for what we were is the kindness of the mind but the heart lives in that which we have yet to become.

Upon a youthful steed that was painted with uniqueness he rode from the darkness into the light one day. Joining others also on life's journey he made his way alone. It was not on any agenda but like riding suddenly upon a field of wildflowers he was overcome by it. It became something he no desire to just pass thru and relish the memory. He wanted to be consumed by it and become a part of the beauty and ecstasy of it. Time after time it would find him capture him again but not to ever last. Saddened by the failure to last, he found himself looking for it with disregard for the randomness that defined it. But yet again he was unable to stay within the comforting arms of it. Many miles he had traveled on his journey and many opportunities he was unable to hold on to. Weary from the journey one day he sought rest and revival at a clear and calm stream. As he looked at his reflection in the clear water he said "It is love I have found and it remains with me forever then why won't it last? Do I not understand how to love?" On his way again but now he had grown accustomed to riding in the shadows as to hide from the fear and forsakenness that now carried him. He had always prayed to god for guidance but this day he prayed for a sign. This day he would come up behind a wagon traveling the same direction as he was. On the back of the wagon were the words the three words beloved to last.

He could tell it was a woman in control of the wagon and he wondered what the words meant to her. As he followed suddenly the wagon lost a wheel and crashed to a stop and throwing the woman to the ground. He looked to see to her safety but she rose before he could reach her. Her hair was long and flowing and her heart shown through her eyes. She smiled as he approached and as she pointed to wagon asked "can u help me?" hesitantly as he looked away from her toward the wagon he noticed the back of the wagon was broken. Where the three words were written was now four words and the now read "be loved to last". The words wandered through his mind until they came together as a thought he softly spoke to himself. "It is not enough to love; I have to be willing to be loved". She heard his voice and asked him "what do you say?" He looked again into her eyes and said "I said it would be my salvation to be of help to you".

SEARCHING, came across the display as the road narrowed and seemed embraced by the trees as they leaned into the path that lay ahead of me. The sun was bright but was playing hide and seek like a child through the dense protective embrace of nature. It had rained earlier and each gift of breath smelled sweeter than the last as if to remind me of the many I had taken for granted. A gentle breeze blew through the tunnel of dancing light with the sun beckoning me onward. Its seemingly random gusts were just enough to shake the moisture from the trees into a cool and refreshing rain. Pavement of man soon gave way to that of nature as the tall grass lay open in front of me. The path sloped down to the edge of a small stream on the edge of an open and vast meadow on the other side. It wasn't deep but deep enough to create a rhythmic and hypnotic sound as all other sounds vanished from hearing. As I looked across the stream a man appeared shielded by the haze of the sun now in its full glory and healing warmth. He appeared to be waving me to come to him. He looked strangely familiar but I couldn't recognize why. As I gently stepped across the stream from on stone to another I could feel the strange sense of electricity pulsing through me from the cool water as it passed through the stones. Once I stepped on the other side I could instantly smell the sour but sweet smell of earth as I felt its cold and healing texture upon my bare feet and between my toes. I walked toward the man still gesturing me towards him and as soon as I came close enough to see him clearly as the sun threw shade upon his face. It was a moment of recognition that filled every empty space within my soul. As my body became one with soul that stood before me I heard a voice from behind me. “You have arrived at the destination within you.”

Whispers of wind occasionally find their way through the wooden screen door. Each wisp traveling a different path than the one before as if each was a lesson to the next. The door remained open leading to this place long forgotten. Each whisper showed itself through the scattered dust clouds and the cob webs filled and bowed under the force across the fireplace mantle. Pictures on the mantle remain hidden and the flame within appears cold and silent from the effects of time. Again, and again the search continues for the light and warmth offered by the gift of life. It was only when the source of wind directed its path that it would discover a fire burning low and hidden by the cold. The coals jumped to life as they reached beyond the chimney in celebration. The power of this celebration drew more whispers of wind through the screen door and this soul of a house danced free from the dust of time forgotten. Each gift of breath we draw should be purposely directed to give power to the fire that lay within us. Peace.

Into the stars I looked with a longing

That among the stars I might walk belonging

I imagine it a place consumed by the light

Where night is day and day is night

Where those stars upon the darkness ride

But in their light, force the darkness to hide

Offering a journey of light constantly in sight

And from the darkness would we never fight

In search of the gift found in peace and light

Like a cloak she wears my heart tear soaked. When there is a chill she holds me close and still. When there is a blush she releases me, careless and rushed. Waiting I remain until again her touch I regain. Knowing it will not last but cherishing the past as an outcast.

Confrontations we don't address remain forever a source of stress.

Her entrance was seemingly unnoticed but hardly unfelt. Cosmic energy drew my glance and once obtained it refused to set me free. The moment was consuming and intoxicating. Everywhere she went I felt the unyielding attraction to maintain her as the focus of my minds eyes. My heart paused in silence as her path led my direction. I remained unacknowledged and invisible as she passed. She came just close enough for the hair on her arm to brush mine.

The touch evoked sensations of endless color and design. The many colors came together to portray a story that only I could read. It was a familiar feeling but the story was unknown to me. Soon it became clear why it felt familiar because my hidden presence was within it. Whether it was a past or future made no difference as the moment stood uniquely on its own. She walked quietly away but the moment now commanded the strength of sorrow as the story came to an end. As she vanished from sight I realized the gift of being reminded that love can exist, even if only for a moment, and nourish the soul in faith.

It came with much effort and sacrifice that I was finally able to silence the voices of the crowd so I could hear my own. With this achievement also comes the ability to isolate all voices in the noisy crowd. All things were just beginning to remain calm and serene as I was able to follow my own voice. Suddenly a voice came from the crowd that was I able to isolate easily. The voice beckoned to me bringing me to a place of past, a place where the noise was loud and selfish. Once you have traveled to the silence of serenity you gain the ability to isolate and hear your own voice as well as the ability to ignore and dismiss any voice from the crowd which does not serve your moment or future.

So, I acknowledged it then I ignored it and left it behind me as I carried only its lesson as a sound unto my heart.

It was merely a hug but it drew us tight.

The power of together we could not fight.

I held her so tight that she began to cry.

And from her strength to trust so did I.

Her tears vanished quickly upon my skin.

Once they gently leaped from her chin.

My tears vanished silently into her hair.

I gently stroked it with repetitive care.

They were not tears evoked of sadness.

They were of joy in the consuming madness.

Passion this deep in tears could be found.

Imagine the joy in smiles we were bound.

As we are forced to experience and accept events bringing loss of what and who was we must realize that what is the end of one form is the beginning of another. Loved one lost in body are found spiritually and walk with us our remaining days until our time comes and then we shall walk together with those yet to find the light.

I felt as though I had seen everything I could possibly benefit from. I had walked so long that everything was familiar to the point I thought I knew what would be next. I took a shortcut back to my car that led to the backside of the expected path. The smell of cotton candy and hay still blew strong in the breeze. I came upon this little tent with a light that was blinking against the shade of the setting sun. It was blinking in a way that I suspected it was not intended for it to blink but it did so because of poor wiring. When the light was on you could read the sign pretty clearly. It said "Dreams $1.00". I was curious and there was no one else around so I stepped through the slit of a doorway leading inside. Inside it was dimly lighted and smelled of some sort of incense. I must have caught them by surprise as I stood there alone and silent for what seemed the longest time. There were pictures everywhere and there were dangly things that dancing and singing different songs as the breeze filled the tent from time to time. I expected to see a table with a crystal ball with a gypsy starring into it, but it was just an open room. Small tables lined the outside and they were covered in books. The books looked, smelled, and felt very old as I fumbled through them as I waited. Between the pictures and books my mind was racing from one subject to another. As I looked at my watch I had been waiting for 30 minutes and no one had come to my attention. I wasn't upset really since I think a person could have spent hours looking through everything. Many of the pictures were of nature settings and very beautiful and inspiring. The inspiration filled me with an energy that insisted I move on so I started for door. The blinking light was now alone in the darkness but it was lighting my way out. Softly from behind me I heard a voice. "Did you find everything you needed?" I was a little confused at first but it made sense pretty quickly as I noticed the little jug with what looked like 5 one-dollar bills in it. I didn't have a one but I felt it was worth the five I dropped in the jug as I left. As I walked to my car I couldn't stop grinning at the thought of how profound the little tent was. Dreams come from within and no one can make them come true but ourselves. All we have to do is believe.

The ice grew thin beneath me as I lost myself in what might have been. She looked longingly upon the vastness of the sea in search of another in her likeness. Each time she would look back to me I could feel her use the warmth in my eyes to dissolve the foundation on which we stood. The day came when the ice would crack beneath me and leave me straddling the divide. In a moments decision I stepped back and the force sent her adrift and free to sail onto her destiny. I watched her crash and collide with others in her likeness until she was lost from my sight. From my accustomed position I turned around and found infinite opportunity in all that was in my likeness. The courage to take the step was a new beginning as hope came alive once again.

I shut my eyes until all I can hear is the sound of the ocean and then I sail everywhere I can take me.

I reflected on the sunset long enough for darkness to overcome me. The day was strong of heat but the evening with the gentle and sporadic breeze was quite calming. Every creature of the night seemed proud to announce their presence. The scent of flowers and trees soon to disappear with the season waited impatiently for the breeze to carry their desperate cries upon the world. The longer I remained the more in tune to the sounds around me I became. I heard the river boat at its peak when passing but paid it no attention. Now that it was fading steadily upon its journey it set my mind in the direction of reflecting those things of the past whose moment had passed. There was a train in the distance and felt its momentum grow stronger and stronger as it came closer and it guided my thoughts to those many things yet to come. The moments under the night sky proved serene but also possessed a sadness of not being manipulated by any urgency or expectation. It was not a sadness of heart but that of mind as we become so busy and isolated from these moments of opportunity when they do reveal themselves we fail to even notice. I listened to the traffic on the highway as each vehicle passed by and noticed that they all sounded similar along their journey. This made wonder if I were any different in the magical scheme of things. Were there others sharing the moments I called my own as their own? It felt comforting to believe we are never alone as we sometime think. I imagined another gathering the same joy from a moment in the darkness and gave eternal meaning to us all being connected and I found even a greater profoundness as I saw the joy on another's face as they shared my peace

When the excuse defines us, it is no longer an excuse but a behavior!

The voice of demon's past beckon to us with whispers so sweet.

Silence is anything but silent once achieved.

Once what seems a long time ago I chased a dream. As I followed it led me to a garden bursting with the colors of the rainbow and a gentle breeze was eagerly sharing the scents of each color. The scents were sometimes individual and then they would evolve as blended gift. The path I followed was narrow and became more so the farther I chased that dream. The path came to an end as it was consumed by entirety of the garden and it all became one connected vision of peace. I dared not go any farther for fear of causing harm by my trespass so I ceased my chase and turned back forlorn and disappointed. Sometime later I returned to the chase of that dream and again found myself at the same garden. With time passing it had grown even more beautiful than I remembered. This time I noticed the sun behind almost pushing me with its warm glow. The dream lay ahead of me just behind a moon so full it filled the sky. Again, I reached the point in the path where it would end and I stopped just like last time but this time in contemplation. I had come to believe that all things were connected and created in the same light. I searched within myself to find that part of me that was flower and as I did I was able to move forward in my chase as a flower, then as a tree, and then as the wind blowing across the sky. On the wind I reached for the moon and caught that dream at last. I could have regretted all the time that passed and seemed lost but then I realized that the time was what brought me to understand that to catch a dream you have to become it.

It was a warm and muggy summer night of my youth. I was lying in the soft green grass gazing up at the clear night sky. As I lay there I was contemplating life I suppose, though my experience and knowledge about it was very limited. In the distance I heard what sounded like a horse running toward me. The sound continued to get louder and closer by my perception. I looked around me but found nothing to explain what I was hearing. Suddenly it just stopped and everything grew silent. Hearing only my own breathing I waited in the silence for it to return. With great surprise I was consumed by a gush of wind. The moon and the stars went dark. The wind was ice cold and sent chills throughout my entire body and soul. As quickly as it came it disappeared and relinquished the night back to warm and muggy. My skin felt drenched but the breeze of warm air now felt cool across my skin. As I looked to the sky the moon was there but all the stars were absent except Pegasus. He seemed brighter than I had ever seen and I starred all the others slowly came into focus as Pegasus blinked its existence. From that day on every time I look upon the night sky Pegasus blinks as if to remind me that anything is possible.

He had been standing at the edge for quite some time but day he stepped off that platform supported by "The Rules". He saddled that machine of independence and freedom and set out in search of the ends of the earth. He was alone and exposed but he found it invigorating and inspiring. The elements of nature were not always kind and considerate of his exposure but at other times they were generous and supportive. Some things he encountered summoned great sadness as he moved past them. Other things were born of sadness and remained as a filter upon his perception. There were moments that he felt he couldn't go any farther and then there were also those moments where he couldn't go far or fast enough. At the moment he reached his destination and thought his journey was over, he realized the ultimate truth. There are no endings but only new beginnings and the joy is in the journey.

From the darkness we hope to be seen. From the silence we hope to be heard. From the perceptions we hope to be understood. From denial we hope to matter. Nothing is exactly as it appears, or is it?

Many times, I sat lost in stare at the portrait of my life. One day it came over me that I should change it. I was not the artist but I quickly dismissed any responsibility, as it was my life portrayed. I added red and it seemed to be full of anger and hate. The only color that would cover the red was black and that brought darkness and sadness upon it. Soon I had made so many changes that the portrait was unrecognizable. It was in this moment I concluded that I was not meant to be the artist but the subject. My only responsibility was to have faith in the true artist.

His expression gave little sign that he had grown used to the bitterness of unshed tears. Each word he spoke in the light flowed ever so slightly tainted by the growing poison within. His heart of a knight forged genuinely as a defender of all that is right. Never even a blink in the light for fear the night would overcome him and his commitment was all that defined him. One day as he stood tall in his routine and ritual he blinked from weariness. In this failure he offered the weakness of his humanity. In that moment he had laid down those weapons of control and protection. He believed his failure would surely and quickly bring harm unto all he felt entrusted to protect and serve. He laid down all his weapons and stood his tallest armed only with his faith. He waited courageously even as his humanity released tears of passion from his eyes. The tears of passion washed away all the bitterness and but left his vision altered. He stood tall and watched through drenched eyes of passion as any and all those he stood against ran from him in fear. He searched for understanding but saw it not. The warmth on his back gained strength as if forcing him to stand down and as he turned the light shined brightly upon him. His tears were dried and his expression came alive as he realized that which he carried faith in would stand taller behind him eternally into the night.

It was in a moment of victory over the relentless adversary of sadness that he acknowledged the beauty of the day. The sun was bright and warming as the clouds, so pure and white, took turns standing before it. At the corner of the horizon their loomed darker clouds but he wasn't sure whether they were coming or had recently gone. As he watched intently to discover their secret he found another secret for which he had not been searching. As the dark clouds were surely moving toward him he had always thought that they pushed the white clouds off the set as the darkness took the stage. Watching like he had not noticed before he saw the dark clouds would simply sneak between the light of the sky and the light in our eyes. Even as darkness seems to consume the brightness remains waiting for the darkness to pass so once again the light can assume the stage of enlightenment. Even when the light of the sun hands off to the light of the moon the clouds of brightness await the suns return and celebrate in colorful majesty. Clouds of dark may come and go but the light remains always bright with faith.

The leaves upon the tree of life are born the color green and growing. There is no race to determine who will be first or last but only a connection in likeness. As the seasons change the circle of connection continues. This juncture does evoke a wonder about first and last and the why that remains hidden. Do they all follow a predetermined path or do they follow the first as it moves beyond the gift of green to discover the completeness found in enlightenment of color. Upon full transition they find release and are carried upon the wind as the journey continues. This true color doesn't change or fade and with purpose adds a new uniqueness to a unified collective. We can resist the transition or we can celebrate the transformation.

Familiarity can be the welcome mat drawing you in the wrong door.

I found myself chasing the pale full moon. Its place in the sky was accented by the thin brow of clouds. The sun was still high in the sky as it warmed my back. Everything that was behind me, disappeared into an orange glow. The past was of no use to me so I chased that moon even harder and took advantage of what lie ahead and made my own path for the secret of my destiny was just to memorize my favorite recipe for happiness.

I welcomed being awakened by the whispers of the fullest of moons as its message seemed magnified as it gently pressed upon the glass of my bedroom window. It would be the start of a day shared by the moon, stars, and sun proportionate to my faith of what they represented. Laughter seemed to always be playing in the background as the wind would perform song after song as the ocean tide would bring magic to the chorus. Of the many faces I can see some are familiar and missed, some are known and cherished, and some are unknown but wished. Sometimes I walk, sometimes I sail, and sometimes I ride, but always I find that which appears in my mind. Peace and love fill the air like humidity but without any drawing heat. The only moisture that escapes this body are tears of joy in the revelation of what should be. Every flower I might touch swells with life that I also can feel as part of the greatest connection in faith. The only sadness I find is in the moment where once again I fall asleep to the sound of an alarm in another room.

Life is not about what we cannot do for others, it is about what we will not do to others.

They were adrift on an open and endless sea. A sea whose depths were as unknown as the limits of the sky that seemed to hold them in place. At first the crew, by the strength of their number, was able to row the vessel of girth. As the days drifted on their number was reduced one by one until their ability in strength was lost. Each one lost was offered to the sea of unknown as the sky watched still silent. One night from the darkness came two voices. The first voice said "Put your trust in me and I will deliver the wind to take you home". The second voice said "have faith in me and I will share a wind that with your help will move you in the direction you need to go". The crew looked to the captain anxiously awaiting and hoping. The next morning the crew stood in position awaiting the captain's orders. The captain waited as well in the silence. Suddenly he took his position at the wheel and commanded the rowers that remained to push forward. With each thrust of the oars the wind purged any slack from the sails. Onward they went until they found their lost lane of travel and continued their journey. A crewman raised his voice over the bellowing wind to ask the captain "what choice did you make?" The captain's answer was whisked away and remains still on the winds of faith.

To seek in gift that which we already possess is to create an endless circle of denial.

I was not lost but with the same breath I was not where I was supposed to be. I had been driving in search of nothingness and I had come far. I passed an old building sitting near the road. It had a single sign hanging on the front. It was faded but still readable it simply said "GROCERY". I felt the immediate urgency to needing a pack of smokes. I contemplated how far I had come in relation to how far it would be if I abandoned my journey and turned back, then fear took control as I imagined what might lay ahead. I found it sad how we cling to those things we think offer protection and comfort even if it's only a pane of glass within a car door. A mile or so ahead I finally overcame the voices of doubt and fear and turned around. As a came upon the store once again, my craving for a smoke became an emergency. I pulled up to the building and after sitting there for what seemed forever checking my phone in disbelief at its response of no signal. I suddenly felt isolated and I have to admit it felt inspiring to no longer feel the pressure to be anything or anywhere. I purchased my smokes from a very kind lady behind a counter that looked like I was only one of many to touch its surface. The inside was so much more unique than the sign eluded. Since I was the only customer in there I looked around awhile and that when I noticed the older gentleman sitting at a desk in the back. He was similarly kind and warm. As they both wished me a good day as I left, the man offered some words of wisdom that I did not immediately understand. I sat in my car now having to face the dilemma of going back or continuing forward. I turned to go forward as the man's words ran clear, "Seek always the unique for your own critique". It was with sadness that I found the interstate three miles ahead.

The treasure of truth does not contain pity so we deny its existence hoping to prolong the search which does.

The catalyst for his revelation was a long-lost love for the wind. It was here that, like us all, he was the author of his own book of life. Each chapter seemingly the progression of the one before it along the preconceived expectations governing the process and thus casting shadows upon the miracle it truly is. With good heart he shared his book one day and the chapters slowly drifted far from once inspired him. As he held tight to the pages unwritten a struggle ensued and the book was tragically torn in half. He was left with only those pages unwritten and memories of those written. The remainder of his book lay on a shelf for what seemed an eternity as he contemplated how to continue it from the blank page that now consumed him. Taking solace in a new wind he was given a thought that made it all make sense. The book of life does not have to be one story but is best depicted as many short stories along our journey. We should find inspiration in the blank pages and live our own story moment by moment or story by story in a series of short stories that explore the endless miracles life has to offer.

Pursue all that you may desire with the appreciation of all that you possess.

With breath so new we find joy in the tiny grip of a finger. With fear of loss we hold tight the hands of youth so precious. With age we find an equal hand to hold in the name of love. With the end we offer our hand in comfort. With adulthood the gift of our hand must be forgotten. With the time passing as sand remember and share the gift of your hand.

The past will be there always to hold our hand but we are still able to reach for the star of choice with faith.

A traveler of time had grown quite fond of the scent of fall. His path evolved from a spinning and shadowing maze to a consistent and intentional following of the colors of autumn. The green gifts of breath stand individually unique. Like multi colored confetti the leaves dance upon the wind until they reach the stage where they dance as a collective of spirits to the next act of their journey. The air is crisp and cool as color becomes part of a stage that will soon welcome new entertainers for our view. As the curtain of white closes, the traveler must get up and move on as we all must do after a fall.

The dawn was so beautiful that is forced him to pull over just to take it in. From the heat of the rising orange sun he found lost inspiration to imagine goals and dreams that he would fulfil someday. As he finished his drive to work his mind raced beyond any posted speed limit. It was a busy day and consumed his thoughts and attention for most of the day. In habit he did manage to sneak off for a quick smoke just in time to the most glorious sunset yet. The setting sun was so large and close, that he could feel its warmth increase as he raised his hand toward it to shade his eyes for a better view. He wasn't long back to work and suddenly felt dizzy, and then darkness. He awakened briefly but perceived it as a dream, as the helicopter blades filled the air. The again he awakened but found no dream as the smell of the hospital room was overwhelming. He spoke to the nurse but was too weak for her to hear. As she drew close he whispered in her ear "Some Day!" don't let your someday be some day!

When the darkness threatens remember that it is chasing the light which always stands behind you.

Whether it is personal or professional relationships, it is not about the walls we build but it is entirely about the walls we maintain. Walls are built under the pretense of keeping things out but the core of their purpose is to keep us in. We want to be kept in that relationship with a significant other or a successful career. Many just want to stay within the area left open from walls. We do not realize that we maintain walls of others from the outside so we may remain unconfined by their environment. Any break in a wall can allow us to fall out or in depending on our desire. If we attempt to exist both in and out we will never realize the potential and success we hoped for. Also, we must consider that if we are trying to tear down walls because we want to move, there will always be those whose actions rebuild from the other side. The key is to find where you belong and maintain the wall of your happiness. Change is hard and time consuming. We have to commit entirely to our choices but be advised to choose wisely.

All I ever wanted to do was live the dream then one day I realized I could only live my own.

He reached out to wipe away that single tear as it searched for its path down her cheek. With his touch the tear simply gave itself over to him as he absorbed the moisture into his hand and suddenly felt drenched in her emotion. He looked deep into her eyes and she knew he understood. He pulled her close and was startled by the collision, as he wasn't expecting her to chase her tear into him. He calmed the beating of her heart and she eased the exaggeration of his breath. No words had been spoken and no names had been exchanged as often happens as we analyze the risk. It is a story of two strangers searching for who they were supposed to be and discovering within another the truth of who they are. The regret found in failure will always pale in comparison to the rewards that are found in risk.

It was a typical weekly adventure and I suppose that I am like many in that I complain but refuse to change. My weekly adventure to Walmart, or at least I use the word adventure to make it sound more exciting. I made my selections following my list which is written in the order the items I wish will appear as I make my journey. This part of the journey is always one that cannot end until I happen across that one item I simply believe I can't live without, given it remains in my budget of course. And if it goes beyond my budget then it gives me something to consume my thoughts over the next week. I head to the checkout, but I only have one option as I was smoker and they are only available at one lane. I pull my cart behind the many ahead of me and immediately pull out my phone to kill the wait time, but what I really hope is that no one will talk to me. I know I'm going to ask for smokes and it is literally a game of battleship to acquire the item I want. Before I even get to the register I am standing on my toes trying to look over the counter and possibly locate the item I want but unsuccessfully and a little embarrassing as I imagine what people wonder what I might be doing. This day as I was standing tall I noticed the lady's name badge at the register. Her name was faith and I felt good about that. When my turn finally came I mentioned her name and said "it must be hard to have a bad day when your name is faith". She replied in the most sarcastic voice ever "I wouldn't know about that!" she was the unhappy person I believe I have ever met. I am still freaking out about having to ask for smokes and it just got worse and the sound of the scanner grew louder and louder it seemed as she worked her way through my selections. The moment came and with great surprise she knew exactly what I wanted and where it was. I thanked her graciously as she helped me put my stuff in my cart. I thanked her again and wished her a wonderful day as I left and she wished me the same and smiled the most genuine smile. As I pushed my wobbling and squeaky cart to my car I pondered a thought. I believe we all need faith but sometimes Faith needs us.

Within the darkness of knight he finds refuge in the silence. Thought by thought he sets aside the armor that hides him from harm. The helmet he wears releases the easiest as it is damp from unseen tears lost into the steel of the mask he wears. This time is short and often unfound. As he replaces his armor he wonders if the weakness and vulnerability can be seen by those he hides it from. Another day he steps up proudly and courageously upon the field of life's battle and continues the remorseful pursuit of his calling. When the moments are most heated he again wonders "would it be better to suffer and survive wounds from the sword of steel or suffer and slowly perish from wounds of the sword of thoughts?" The only armor of thoughts is truth.

The moment the sun became a pencil line across the horizon that lay in front of her she sprang from hiding and ran toward the orange line below the dark sky. She heard the monster behind her in the darkness stir, and she knew it would give chase. She was running with everything she had but she couldn't stop looking back. She couldn't see anything behind her but her thoughts betrayed that truth with deceptions of imagination. The darkness behind her was fading away into the light except when she looked back, and then it seemed to lunge forward to her. Looking back, she suddenly tripped on something and rolled to the ground and lay there looking for the darkness. She was trembling with fear but could not move. As she lay there she could see the sun pushing back the shadow and she frantically hoped it would reach her before, but WAIT!

One direction dark gray with danger and another direction light gray with hope. Neon pierces the darkening sky and voices fill the empty air. People you don't or will ever know steadily move along with urgency while you remain oblivious but observant. The street lights change color in rhythm even when there is no one to even see it, let alone abide by the implied directive. Is that perhaps the secret of life; seeing the implied directive. What if peace is hidden by the neon pretending to create the light of day?

I feel the sound of the rumble within me
I hear the echo of the wind passing me
I chase the sky where the sun teases me
I become lost in this world of only me

I know when the end comes for me
I will tremble and shake beyond me
I will know the journey has changed me
I imagine that life is much like
Working through traffic on my bike
Yearning for the open and serene
But patient till the red turns green
On red I must set my feet on ground
And hold my place steady in the crowd
With green I start anew once more
Drowning out red with a green roar
Off again I search for places unknown
And fear will become courage in known
Witness of my travels may be me alone
But none can take away that I have flown

I was driving into the sunset this evening and it was beautiful beyond words. I pulled over so I could savor in the moment. My first thought that I was lost in it but the truth is I was found in it.

Those unimportant things in life grew silent and the calm and serene easily sorted out anything negative that might remain. As I imagined its existence a gift to only me I just happened to glance in the rear-view mirror. I was so caught up in the beauty I had always failed to notice its affect beyond me. The pink tinted clouds behind me drifting on a sea of blue compelled me to realize that just because we don't see it does not mean it is not there. Abandon the selfishness and embrace the place we share as part of everything.

If you look to the past to heal your future you will only poison your present.

You are one of these families of ours.
Connected like the night sky stars.
When things may dim your light.
We turn to you throughout your plight.
We offer our light and stand.
As our way of holding your hand.
Rest assured that your prayers and thoughts.
Become our wishes for miracles sought.

If you want to keep the merry-go-round spinning you have to put a foot down and help. The longer you wait, the harder it becomes. If you want to go the other direction you have to wait until it is completely stopped and start again. Choose wisely, lol.

You see limitation by the perceived definition where I see limitless definitions.

Blue hair is greatly enhanced by the blue glow of the fly light. We seem not to even acknowledge the tirade of death that exists around us. Try as we may to remain lost in our own thoughts in search of peace we are constantly brought back. We are brought back by the voice whose desire is to announce each and every thought and action at the octave just beneath screaming. We become lost but not in a reality of choice but in a reality of service to others who deny we even exist. Oh well. Back to the blue haze of reality.

Miracles are visible in the average as well as the extraordinary if we look for them instead of waiting for them to show us.

The tree of life will more generously yield fruit when the soul, mind, and body see the same reflection in the water of the river that feeds it.

Find inspiration from your action and not from their reaction.

Those who always seem to fly do so because they learned how to fly without even considering ever landing.

Each day shall bring whatever it must but in the lessons of yesterday we find our trust.

The heart feels without the minds permission. A glance that erupts with energy into a purposeful stare. Only when he felt too close to being caught he would look away and then chastise himself for doing so. The heart couldn't be choosing by looks as he never made it out of the depth of her eyes. Could it be that he sensed her soul beckoning to him for recognition? Could two hearts introduce and recognize one another before the minds could give the command to see. Once commanded to see he would look upon her as the surroundings moved in recognition of her presence. Her hair long and flowing with a darkness matching her deep ocean eyes. He became lost within her and overcome by the wondering the truth of her being. He felt that he was never caught invading a space in which his mind had yet to feel welcomed. His heart on the contrary was comfortably at home. Perhaps she had caught his invasion and was feeling the same. He knew not how to cross this boundary between heart and mind so from the distance his heart was the sole explorer in a newly discovered land. His heart would race as the air carried her to the door. His mind simply waiting for a sign it could understand. The sign did not come and she vanished from sight but she will remain forever and always touched by the heart.

It's impossible not to stare but the line runs thin between staring and attraction. The latter is uniquely more appropriate. Her dark eyes capture you and pull you in without mercy. When you struggle to free yourself and succeed all you can wonder is why. Her long dark hair ending in curls and each one more perfect than the other. She walks with such grace that it seems air itself steps aside so as to not disturb perfection. She seats herself and her legs cross before resting. She slips off her shoes to expose her bare feet gently crossed. As she eats she looks to enjoy each bite like nothing she may have enjoyed before. Her joy expresses itself even through her bare feet as she extends and arches her food with each morsel she would consume. Consumed it exactly what emotion she arouses by her mere existence. Then as suddenly as she controlled you she slips away with the stern look from the man across from her. But it too late as you have already intimately experienced the beauty within her.

Scantily obscured by the dark blue cloak of bitterness, the light becomes so focused that it displays its intenseness in colors of red, true and pale. The light stands its ground despite the shadows always moving in an effort to overcome it. The bitterness is always the strongest when it first appears, after a long absence. The light will always prevail and so shall we if we chose to stay with the light instead of chasing the darkness. The message is profound that we can learn from a sky that says snow tonight but sunny tomorrow.

The chill of winter can linger and grow for days or a lifetime. Layer by layer we build our defenses but bitterness only strengthens its isolated and trapped hold upon us. Even the slightest wisp of warmth intensifies the desperation. Silent and still we wait for relief that we know will never come. It is in a moment of despair that we realize that the warmth we seek comes from within. Layer by layer we expose ourselves to the harshness. As the chill within us becomes vulnerable we realize its true strength growing within. A defense that isolates also eliminates the warming exchange of passion.

Day by days that lead to year by years I traveled this same road. It has become a habit of convenience in hopes that it will lead me where I need and want to go. One week this past summer as I was traveling this road and I came to the forever red light, I noticed an old man sitting on the curb at the light. This is one of those red lights that you almost pull out into traffic to make sure you have triggered the light to change to green but never seems to matter. All but the last day of my work week he was just sitting there. The light takes so long that it became uncomfortable as I imagined him staring at me. On my Friday he was there again but this day

I decided to talk to him. As the light turned red as it always did I looked to the curb and he wasn't there. It was a warm day so I had my window down. To my surprise he stepped up to my window. I quickly looked at the light as if it was close to changing but I knew it wasn't. "Can I ask you a question sir?" he said. I said I don't know it takes me where I want to go and I am familiar with it. "Have you ever considered another road?" he again asked. I said no not really, why? As I turned to hear his answer he was gone but a horn from behind me warned that the light had turned green and I went on my way. On my next work day, I looked for him. I came to a stop at the red light, but he was nowhere to be seen. As the light turned green and I made the turn I was confronted by road closed signs blocking the road. There was no warning about the road being closed. I stared at the signs and for a moment contemplated going around them. I always leave early and that was good since now I had to find a new road. I did find another road and it was much better. It had no stop lights and it offered the greatest view of the sunrise to start my day with inspiration. After about a month of using this new way I saw that old man standing on the side of the road holding a sign. He smiled and waved at me as I passed him. His sign said "trust your signs".

From the sanctity of my room with the covered windows I pushed my way through the resistance of the door. I was immediately exposed to the blinding and yet enlightening light of the sun reflected by each and every flake of snow. The air I breathe was silent, still, and bitter cold. There were no sounds other than the sound of the snow compacting upon itself, not unlike myself when I succumb to my inner thoughts. I stood there on my porch unable to move. I felt unable because with each movement I risked the bitter cold touching an unadjusted place upon my skin and perhaps within my soul. Each breath became slow and distant to avoid the sting of coldness, but I believe it was nature's way of encouraging me to remain in this place I had stumbled upon. The longer I remained the more it felt like that time just after my work day is done and I lay down to sleep in preparation for the next day. This place where time stands still and the demands of me grow weak. In this place truths become clearer and the true meaning of life becomes visible. It is here that time is without rules as even a second can carry the wisdom of years. It is with sadness and with a renewed sense of purpose I step from the porch to carry on my day. And though the moment is lost I will remember and revisit this place known as the present. Only in the present can the past and future be rendered powerless.

The lonesome howls of life were beckoning me today to come out and play. They remind me that the most important lessons taught are those of moments sought. As I ventured into the arena, the sun was blinking at me from beyond all the things we use to hide ourselves away. It felt like a recognition and appreciation of my presence. Openness is what I sought and the sun led the way. The wind today did not need any encouragement from me and was quite boisterous and determined. Quickly I discovered that the wind would be a powerful friend or foe in my quest. The words 'Go where the wind blows" came to mind but my perspective was to use the wind to take you where you want to go. As I held steady against the winds wishes and stood my ground I found that it pushed me faster and farther as the sun pulled me closer and closer. It was like sailing the highway of life and the resistance only made it more rewarding. Between the gusts I was still able to find that silent and serene place in my mind where I organized my thoughts and swiftly let go of those that didn't serve me unto the wind. I knew I would never catch the sun but the joy comes from the journey of hope. I shifted weight on my sails and turned around and headed back with the sun at my back. Slowly the openness gave way to the comfort of all things hidden. This time in my final stretch it was the darkness that winked at me as if to show its compassion for a traveler home safely. A game well played always produces pride even if it's merely a bike ride.

Maggie's clouds were full and had nowhere to go but as drops gliding gently and silently down her cheeks. Each one was following the forged path of the others before it. Soon the repetitive rhythm caused her eyes to close and she drifted away into a dream she had come to know well. She was strangely awakened this time by the soft touch of a woman kneeling next to her, wiping away the one tear that refused to follow the same path and stood alone. Maggie opened her eyes that were still moistened with sorrow, to find herself again in a hallway. It was the same hallway that she had seen many times but something was different this time. The woman said "My name is Mary. Why do you remain here?" As Maggie looked around she asked Mary "What happened to all the closed doors?" "Maggie the only closed doors are the ones you put there. This place has always been about doorways. These doorways are specific and uniquely your choices. You continue to knock on the doors you have created awaiting a welcoming and invitation. You don't need permission to enter any doorway any more than you need to knock on any door in your own house." Mary slowly drifted away and disappeared into one of the doorways and in that moment Maggie truly awakened and wiped that one tear from her cheek.

The sea of disappointment is best sailed with the present winds of encouragement. Past winds serve only the anchoring amidst the journey.

The demons of expectation often lead us into the clouds of chaos. On one such day I turned quickly as the clouds suddenly changed direction and led me at their beckoning. I was startled as I turned to see a man standing in front of me. Before I could ask who, he was or where he came from he said with a hint of humor, the winds of change. The sky behind him was the blue and beckoning. I again turned to see if the clouds had cleared but they remained and as quickly as he had appeared he had now vanished. He was gone but I would be the beginning of many encounters yet to come. At every sunrise and sunset, I looked upon he would appear. He never spoke but always seemed to know what I was thinking and how I felt in the moment. His expression always seemed to mimic my thoughts. At work when I would gaze through the window of thought he would be there grinning. Every bike ride I would see him waving at me as I traveled. With every friend or unique new acquaintance, he would always be there paying close attention. I didn't realize the pattern at first but later I realized that he was always there when I was confidently and honestly just being me. It was here that I finally understood that he was the image of my true self and there to guide me to those things that accepted me freely. I had found myself and with each encounter grew stronger of mind. Life is a passion of choice.

It was so long ago that he covered the windows to his soul. The reasons have changed and evolved with time in a feeble attempt to validate the feelings which drew the blinds. With his ear to the threshold he listens for signs of hope. The sound of a breeze whistles a memorizing tune that paints the pictures with the colors of his imagination. Often, he wonders how the windows must look from the other side but neglects to notice in his haste to travel beyond and return to the presence of safety he has built. The things the threshold promises become silent and hidden to eyes that won't see. Day by day the travels are corrupted with only thoughts of return. One day he hopes to see those windows that are covered and open them from beyond to allow his truth to be seen clearly. One day he hopes to take the moment and listen upon the threshold from beyond and realize that it offers only silence and sadness. It will be in this brief moment of thought that he will release weight of the armor he wears and accept life for what it is. "It is what it is" is dependent upon our choice of it.

Night after night after night he struggled falling asleep. As soon as he would shut his eyes a piercing light would beckon him through closed lids. He covered windows and turned out all sources of light but it remained. If he opened his eyes to expose this source of penetration it was nowhere to be found. It was not a constant light but similar to a light house or river boat. That similarity only adds mental calculation and anticipation to further block or postpone sleep. The door to that magical dreamland would eventually open and close behind him but not without a fight, it seemed, every night. One day as he was talking of this dilemma with a friend an older woman sitting nearby spoke up. "What's your hurry honey? I imagine you go to bed for the purpose of getting up. You go to work for the purpose of coming home and you come home to go to bed and start all over again. Just because you think you can tell time does not mean you can control it. Life is about moments and they happen at their own pace. That's not a lighthouse you see, it is the rising and setting sun spinning at the speed you attempt to enter that world and it won't have it. Eventually it will slow you down so that it can show you what you need to see, whether you understand it or not. Slow down and enjoy the world as it comes to you." Her words kept echoing in his head the rest of the day and he found her words to seem true as he watched the sunset for the first time in a long time. That night as he lay down the light was there again but this time it was clear it was a sunrise that he could only imagine. He could feel the warmth of the sun on his face and see the shade of pink his eyelids became as he mentally gave in to this worlds power and magic. The next morning, he awoke with a renewed sense of purpose and priority. Set yourself free.

The poorest of carpenters we must be as the walls we build never have windows.

The gift of wondering is best served, not about why things happen but why they don't.

Isn't it sad that we don't know where we are going but we never forget how to get back?

All the faces hint all the stories

Some familiar and some so distant

Smiles hide eyes darkened of worries

Interaction colors the dark in an instant

With color some evolve in positive fury

And some glow quietly but hesitant

The quiet are calm in observance of furies

The furies contemplate the resistant

Each its own but the group is blurry

Until you step back to see the moment

We are all one in the entire story

Growth is never more evident as when we can travel beyond the storms painted by memories and see new colors in the rainbow.

The rain begs our attention with its collective sound.
Taking over the silent stillness in the darkness found.
Seemingly in a world in which on and off it's bound.
But searching the collective uniqueness can be found.
How the journey of each raindrop can be so profound.
Some join another and some wait patiently to be found.
Some fade quickly and some remain alone to the ground.
Between the on and off there is inspiration to be found.
It is in the state of pause that we find that miracles abound.
But why we dismiss the pause is truly a topic to confound.
Seek your souls pause and allow life to truly astound!

What if reality is just label we use to describe something we don't understand? Most of us sleep at night and live during the day. We hear quotes about another chance that called tomorrow. What if life is not about a number of days we claim as ours? What if life is just that "A LIFE"? The sun we see is life with wide open eyes. The moon we see is life as it blinks. The storms we endure are life when it cries. We work toward our destiny, only to give up and start again in our perceived new day. The body needs rest but the mind stays true. Imagine if we lived our life as if it were a story that we couldn't stop reading. Even in sleep we could let our dreams continue our quest and waste no time, if it truly exists, in our life so precious and unique. Tomorrow as we call it is not promised and yesterday is gone. All we truly have is now and isn't that what life is supposed to be "now"? Awake or asleep our journey continues blink after blink after blink. Take notice of your blinks and you will find no pause, so why does life have to follow "Just because".

The eyes deceive. The mind concedes. It's the heart that beats the contemptuous drum of truth.

Words outspoken only reflect the mirrored images of all that we already know we are and do.

Change is found in the words spoken within to unlock all that we can be or do.

Good days are not a gift, they are a creation.

He searched and searched for words that soothed
But found instead the words that moved
In them was a strength he had to share
For any other whose soul lay bare
To discover that the best soul soothing

Is found in things best at soul moving
I find myself dreaming as I lay awake, dreams of sleeping
where I can truly awaken

He searched for an answer to the pain he felt. The search itself was a struggle as he kept wondering outside the box that was the task. Could it be or should it be this easy? Maybe it's not even real but merely an alarm the body sends to warn of an approaching edge, or a wrong road. Once again to regain focus on the search amid the spinning thoughts, he found nothing defined by the pain he felt. Reading over and over and further and further but nothing matched how he perceived it to be prescribed. Abandoning the search, he returned his list to his pocket and felt the beating of his heart as it raced without his knowledge. The beats from his heart drummed out the sounds of his mind chattering. The rhythm played on and on until it became such a calming tone. It was in this calmness that he found a truth in the quote "the heart and the mind are allies and opponents on the same team but only both working together will produce victory." The night air and sky seemed so fresh as the automatic doors guided his path. He wondered "Why doesn't Advil offer a selection for a life headache?"

The sunset had faded and the sky grew dark. The moon was full and bright but cast an opalescent glow upon the night. He was awakened by a noise and quickly noticed his world all aglow. He peeked from behind a brown curtain that now was illuminated of white. He saw nothing to explain the noise but quickly noticed the strange moon light. Then he noticed on his porch table something that looked like a book, but he had not left it there. Cautiously he crept past the front door, looked all around as if he would find someone there. No one was there but the book still lay on the table. It looked to be a very old book by the way its cover was worn and in raised text the cover read "Book of Dreams". He opened the book but it gave no clue like most books do. He found one story after another. He read the first few lines of the first story and found it intriguing so he thought he would save that story and check out the next. Story after story he passed until he reached the last one and as he turned that page it only read "story of your life". He felt very confused as he continued page after page but all were blank. As he gave up on that last story he felt ok because he had passed oh so many that he knew he would enjoy. As he flipped back to the beginning he became alarmed as he found all the pages were now blank and the book was empty. Only the cover title remained. A cloud drifted past the moon and his porch grew dark but when the moon reappeared the book was gone. He looked around but found nothing to see. His whispered to himself the last story in the book “Story of your life”. He didn’t understand who or why this message was sent but he understood the messages intent. Live each moment as it comes along because once you pass it there is no going back.

I’m not sure which hurts more, jumping back and forth over that fence or how it drags against my arms as I go.

As I ponder the saying "forget the past and move on" I think what if. What if we are supposed to plan our future to build a past we won’t regret but cherish when our time comes to remain there.

Release those ties that bind

Travel light in sprit and mind

Say no goodbye's but only hellos

Trust the circle of life as it flows

It is amazing what can happen with the sewn seeds of possibility when they are tended.

He held the balloon tightly within his hand and heart. He enjoyed watching and learning as it danced in the wind and rose again every time it would fall. Then he noticed how it tugged at his hand yearning to be free. He feared the loss but was anxious as to the possibilities he might witness. He released it and it quickly rose into the sky with a freedom he could feel. He silently chased the balloon along its journey and found wonder in how it was perceived by others. Some knew what it was and stared imagining the beauty. Others found different perceptions that he had not even considered. He chased until it lost to his sight but it remained in his imagination of flight. He wondered if it would ever fall but chose to believe it continues still, imparting its freedom for all to see. All who might find value and wisdom within his act of sharing his heart with a simple red balloon?

It was just an old coat. I had been wearing it for the longest time. In time I did come to notice how it didn't look the same as it once did. I also found that it did not protect me from the elements of life as I hoped. It was worn with wear and torn from despair. It had become so comfortable over time that I found it hard to wear anything new. At times I felt the embarrassment I was sure it drew by its failings to conceal and protect. One day when my courage was strong I shed that coat in a fury of thought. To my surprise I noticed that old coat was designed to be worn on both sides. As I pulled the sleeves the rest of the way through and turned the collar around I slipped that old coat back on. All the worn, torn, but comfortable aspects I now wore on the inside and from the outside it looked changed and new. I no longer felt ashamed of my worn and weathered life as the comfortable moments now remained with me inside that old coat. So, if you too might feel vulnerable and yet by the past bound, just turn your coat around.

In a distant past there was a moment filled with the greatest of faith. For from that moment sprang the greatest of days. It was a beginning or perhaps a continuing, per divine intervention. A seemingly solitary journey until you imagine it as stars crossing paths and thus never the same. The way flowers bloom at the passing of a breeze or maybe her gentle hand. A journey marked by the width of its affect as opposed to any predetermined destination. Another moment along the way gave birth to another who might recant this tale of magic and mystery. Another whose journey like many others a star-crossed gift of love and light. Life is about the moments and a single moment can be celebrated again and again and each time with more appreciation for the flowers that bloom. Happy Birthday Mom. Love you much.

Miracles can be defined as happenings without expectation but with limitless expectation, happenings become a way of life.

The bitterness in the wind encouraged the dull ache of anticipation. The colors all in bloom would gladly offer moments of appreciation. The reflective blue sky holding the sun as its prize brings warmth to soul's expectation. Spring is such a magical temptress of acknowledgement.

The scent of honeysuckle dances to its own music gently upon the breeze. The heat of the day can be quickly undone by the chill of the shadows and the shade. Every moment forward brings divine clarity and understanding in the reflection of moments gone by. There are no signs and facing the unknown with courage is to truly fly. As one's focus becomes less defined we become able to see the entire image of life as it is and not as we are led to believe. I have no desire to land and nor the will to surrender my path amongst the clouds for one of limiting definition. Choose not the perception you're given but embrace the perception that you see.

Taken back by a clear rejection.

Nowhere to be found in my perception.

But from back my path became a clear election.

And in those choices, I find perfection.

To speak the words your heart must hear.

Is to dismiss the mind's irrational fear.

The mind believes it is the protection.

But merely defends the heart's projection.

I crave a moment that will begin as an eternity. An eternity that is merely a single breath in time. Courage will fall like a sudden summer rain as I become engulfed in the possibility of the moment. The lips so soft as we mingle in exploration. The touch of her face makes my fingers so heavy. The kiss will fade into a tight embrace that bonds the souls no longer strangers. The fire of passion melds us even closer as I lose myself in the scent of her hair only to dream another dream.

The winds of change are always whistling the most alluring tunes. Their tone is surprisingly the loudest on the calmest of days. It was a day such as this in addition to being unseasonably mild and brought a chill to calmness that abounded. She was greatly affected by the silent allure but could find no vision as she paced back and forth over the same spot from whence she came. She could not seem to bring herself to step away from the large tree under which she paced and took refuge. A wise owl that lived in the tree, which her pacing was disturbing as he napped under the warmth of the afternoon sun, flew down just in front of her. Quickly he spoke as he knew she would run back in fear. "What is it you seek that keeps you trapped in the same spot?" After a moment of shock, she said, "My yellow brick road". The wise owl chuckled but tried to restrain the humor he found in her answer. He said the yellow brick road is a metaphor for your own road no matter where you take it. Surely you don't believe your path is guided by child's nursery rhyme?" she gave the hint of a grin and said no of course not, that would be like believing owls could speak." The wise owl bowed his head slightly to acknowledge her point and with one outstretched wing he stood aside and ushered her on her way. As she walked past him he said "I believe you're on your own way."

Regardless the perspective which voices the constant barrage of unmet expectations it still alters ones path to one of discouragement. When things that happen to go correctly are ignored and only the failings gain attention it forces the question "what's the point?" A mere number among many is a sad and unsatisfying choice of life. Can we be any more corrupted than we are as to the true purpose of existence? The rich get richer and the poor get poorer with no revelation of worthiness in sight. It is said that if you help enough others to get what they want and you will get what you want. I find this to be a never-ending battle in which bitterness grows and conquers the giving soul as he is misled to believe those we help will return what we give. Life is all about which lie we choose and how we validate that decision as good for the soul of the giver.

Every day he defeated the overwhelming urge to run. But what he could not defeat was whether he would be running from or to something. Every place he saw that appealed to his every sense became a dream of his place in the sun. And then the sun would shine upon him where he stood and the reasons to run slipped away with the setting sun. He thought perhaps he wasn't meant to run but walk to many places that would enrich his soul along his journey. He contemplated the difference between a place that offered work and life as opposed to one that might offer life and work. Often it is said that one must find happiness from within as anything else would leave one longing for something they haven't the vision to see. In his mind he searched the horizon set afire by the setting sun for answers but it didn't give up anything except the darkness filled with stars and a full moon to keep him company as he pondered all that lay within. Maybe it's not answers we seek but the understanding that we are a part of something infinitely larger than ourselves.

It could be said that the abandonment of humanity is to discover it.

Regardless the results, the mind believes it makes our choices along our journey. But all the mind does is resist the decisions the heart can't change. The mind that has faith in the heart will be free from the debt of regret.

To take offense to words of hate is to manifest the emotion of hate without so choosing. Choose carefully the words your mind accepts and your true emotions you will never fear losing.

My heart has gone, giving no notice, no baggage in hand.
It follows no rhyme, offers no reason, and will hear no fight.
My mind must analyze under the distraction of the hour glass sand.
Because it knows fear despite the trust that the heart is always right.
The mind looks longingly but remains hesitant where it stands.
The only link between the two is the silent voice in the night.
Of the soul torn between the two as it suffers every grain of sand.
Waiting until once again they can be one traveling upon the light.

All the colors you see with your eyes shut tight are the same colors you see when u look into the light.

Storms build silently on sunny days but it's the storm that produces the sunniest of days.

Interaction by thought can paint the most beautiful picture but it disappears once you look away from it.

The question of when will it be over will only be answered when you stop asking.

With rhyme my mind wishes to impart
The deepest convictions of my heart
In the reflection upon my life's start
And every single step across the chart
Of my journey thankful for your part
Even from boy to man did I depart
Your soul's echo and I never apart
Your reflection always guiding my heart
Your example filling my sails keeps me on chart
With gratitude I shall always be indebted to you

Time moves so slowly as the answers to questions came so freely but moves so quickly when answers resist. In this paradox the truth is that the answers are always with us but it's the questions we must seek.

The paths we take that are not by choice will not feel right at the end unless we can see the beauty of the journey in spite of the thorns.

Most people walk thru life like they walk the isles of the grocery store without a list. Peace Self-liberation is not a festive event with applause and fireworks; it is the subtleness of a sunrise but not for what you see but what you look for.

Life is a place I visit often but briefly as a traveler but home will always be the place called living.

It is from weakness that we discover the courage within us and it is from courage that we remember the weakness that defines us.

The wind just suddenly gave up its journey. It was replaced by the sound of every sail on the ocean of life falling to its lowest achievement all at once. Then the wind began again after merely taking a breath to blow stronger. The sound of the sails once again taking flight drowned out the sound of the winds next surge. Focus not on the wind to yet come but your readiness to fill your sail with the knowledge that lowest is lowest but highest has no limit.

Sometimes letting go means to discover you weren't holding on but being held on too.

Some people only feel they exist when turbulence brings them up from the sands of time.

One might think life is about being tested but it's more about preparedness. One must always keep the faith. One must always believe things happen for reasons beyond our understanding in foresight and become clear in hindsight. One must be always willing to participate in the choices life offers. One must always keep trying without losing appreciation for what blessings exist. One must understand that life opens doors but will not push you through them. One must not wait out the rain for the sun to shine. One must accept life as a book being written page by page to reveal the best of you.

Tormented by choice is far more detrimental to change than choosing poorly.

Everywhere I turned the signs were there saying you can't get there from here. I wondered how they even knew where I wanted to go but no matter as it is impossible to get there from here, one must go there to get there.

How would you celebrate the completion of roads you never wanted to travel? You don't, you celebrate the opportunity to try again.

Blind are those who refuse to see

Invisible are those who refuse to be

Lost are those who are quick to flee

Found are those who discover the key

Is to sail beyond the boundaries of your sea

Dare to go or stay, the decision is in to dare.

The many fingerprints on the dusty window blinds of life inspire hope in that we are not alone. Peace

The day had arrived and the butterflies consumed me but it was the whisper of joy their wings were singing that kept all other thoughts at bay. The people waited in attendance but I could not see their faces because I had only one face on my mind. The music started but it was lost to the music from the butterflies as they led me with their sounds of pending climax. I glanced at the dress and took in her beauty but quickly became lost in her eyes and soul. She grasped my hand and the music subsided to the sound of a distant voice. I followed along as best I could but I could hardly wait to speak I do. The next words I remember are a bold you are. The butterflies took flight to music once again and as we walked I knew we would no longer walk as two but fly as one. And this is the story merely titled "the little things".

The doors in life are plentiful but if you insist upon standing in front of one door waiting for it to open you will miss out on the opportunities that openness offers.

We will never be the right one as long as we hold on to the wrong one.

Many a sunset I vowed to witness and many I have been blessed to see. Then one day I noticed how the setting sun slows down just before it disappears as if it awaits me to follow in spirit so that I may truly see and understand the blessing of peace.

The dust of a windless day remains illuminated in the closing shards of sunlight but the moon does glow as if it's all alone without any hint of its borrowed light but in harmony they do exist.

The best chapter in our book of life will be just a memory when we stop writing. One must appreciate the good with the bad but your story is never over unless you allow it to be.

Starting over is not nearly what it implies
And the truth is hidden by all the lies
By definition starting reluctantly complies
To anything more than once it denies
Starting over is continuing on in disguise
And continuing on one will quickly realize
It is about fitting into a story we can idealize
And accept another's history as we rationalize
The blending of two paths that might harmonize
Into a collective goal they can visualize.

Drifting clouds so sinister and gray
Steal away the last light of the day
Strong and bright will have last say
Setting crimson fire to those that may
Allowing beauty to keep darkness at bay
Always looking and it shall never stray
As positive will always find a way

Between each page of any tale
We imagine how the next will sail
Maybe we encounter winds that prevail
Maybe into the unknown we continue to sail
Either way the tale winds continue to wail

Lean it hard into the curves

If you want where you deserve

Keep your eyes on the road ahead

As eyes on curves bring much dread

Curves of life are part of your story

Use them and find your greater glory

If you always assume no then disappointment will linger with you always but if you assume yes then disappointment is fleeting as it surrenders to surprise.

A single orange burst barely seen

Against the comfortable hue of green

A discreet sign of pending transition

Most often met with much opposition

But I don't mind the change at all

That brings the fierce colors of fall

The grandest tree of oak aspired to that grandeur by surrounding itself with branches and leaves of the inspired.

The journey of life can be a mirror of many stories. As readers we dwell in the reflections but as writers we choose the projection.

I gaze so intensely into the fire of the setting sun hoping to become part of it. Some might say I look lost but I am truly found. In those final moments as the fire fades forward it casts light on everything behind me. It is in this teaching display I remember that as I move on and forward all that lay behind me was with purpose and profound intention.

He who desperately searches for a quality in others will find it in everyone.

He who listens to the qualities of everyone will find those unique to one.

A moment of rest on this rock I wonder
How many shared this seat of ponder
I do my best to take in the precious view
longer I look the more my spirit renew
The scale is greater than can be seen
The vision instilled is wonderfully serene

An aspiring journey is merely an outline and only receives the colors of life when we believe we deserve and take ownership of our aspirations.

The mental picture that inspires your goals should not be of how to start but more importantly how to finish.

The pages of life are so easily read and reread. It is in turning the pages that we must find our greatest strength and desire.

The corridors were crimson and smelled of lavender
No signs of destination but music suited to meander
The shadows fell in front of me as along I did wander
Light within me offering infinite possibilities to ponder

I had often wondered if I were a creature of habit or perhaps one of commitment. Most of the time I would just let it go with just being a creature. I work what seems like every day and drive the same route to work and at the same time of day. I don't choose the shortest route as I enjoy the little space with a sense of freedom. My route takes me across a little section of wilderness that is definitely less traveled, except for me I suppose. There is only one house I can see toward the end of this serene and silent getaway. Every day I see woman walking toward her mailbox to get her mail. She is walking everyday no matter the weather and even on Sunday. I can't say much about Sunday as I walk to my mailbox on Sunday as well pretending in my mind that I didn't get it the day before. One day as I drove by her I noticed she was digging a hole and her mailbox was beside her in preparation to be placed in the new location further away from where it was previously. My first thought was how weird it seemed, and then I realized that I was driving by her every day so I just accepted it without understanding. Day after day and week after week she continued with this mailbox moving ritual until her mailbox was almost at the opposite end of the road from where her house was. I mean it was the only house I could see so I assumed it was hers. One day toward the end of this summer I saw her walking and I slowed down just beside her. I say slowed because even as I came within speaking distance she just continued walking. I asked her if she needed a ride, but I knew it was a ridiculous question given society today, but I suppose foolish and heard is better than foolish and silent. She did turn my way and graciously turn down my offer. Well I was there now and I didn't want to let it go so I asked her, while still driving beside her on the wrong side of the road, why she kept moving her mailbox farther and farther away from her house. At this question she stopped, turned toward me and totally consumed me with her dark eyes in anticipation. She said "It is in the space between what we think and what we see that courage is born. The amount of space is different for everyone but you were about to run out of road." Now we share a mailbox and walk together.

The poetry we might seek to achieve
Evolves from that we might believe
Sadness and joy as we might perceive
But together offer a poet's reprieve

Often when you chase the sun
It's from a storm you must run
It's the light that gets our attention
But the rain is divine intervention
Freedom is found not in avoidance
But fearless in the acceptance
And learn that from deviation
Is found our greatest appreciation

I see you moon no need to act so shy
Hiding among clouds in a pale blue sky
Even though your light is soft and thin
I know the potential of your light within
Teaching your lesson that I make mine
It's not about how bright but just to shine

The smell of the burning exhaust is better than any perfume to claim me.

An aroma that is there when I stop to remind me of the blessing life can be.

As I ride alone my chosen path free in tune with me and all the powers to be.

I see the sun and I see the moon

Both so bright and full in bloom

Once I thought they could never meet

Yet thru me is perceived a dance so sweet

The things we do and convince ourselves we must shall be of little consequence when we must return to the dust.

The cause in hindsight will lay in the prevention.

Policy and procedure are merely the means of retaining control but how and when you use the control determines your success or failure.

To feel pain without her even uttering its name
To feel the sorrow without need to escape to tomorrow
To feel pleasure without any need to apply measure
To feel joyfulness when one soul be lost in hopelessness
To be so at peace in knowing the circle will never cease
Is to defy the separateness and embody the togetherness

Cumbersome thoughts of wish and worry
Never find an ending to their ironic fury
As our ruled notecard becomes so blurry
Feeling behind and start again in such hurry
But when we stop looking at the lines of injury
We find we are our own judge and jury.

To spend the present pursuing justification of the past will surely ensure the future to be no more than the past repeated.

The words escape me but the thoughts remain.
Even when expression is tangible the outcome shall remain the same.
As thought is premature, words are late and in vain.
But such is life for the hopelessly mundane.

The public today is more often just shitty

When u get down to the nitty gritty

They demand a unique perfection be given

And yet they are far from perfection driven

They never speak of anything that's right

But complain with the intensity of a fight

Threats and belittlement in distraction

As if we are not capable of satisfaction

But in the end, I suppose they feel strong

By calling out to everything so wrong

But our secret of perfection is preserved

In our knowing its perceived not deserved

Love is silent and accepting with no need for validation.

Hate is violent and condemning but requires participation

The most beautiful sunset settles beneath a starlit sky so wide.

The perfect ocean wave settles into the changing tide.

The perfect sunrise loses its glory beyond the settled horizon where it hides.

The sand in the hour glass of time settles as memories in our mind.

Should relationships be always seeking a different high or find contentment in the settling kind.

Cursed are they who look through eyes that don't see age for they are only seen by eyes that gauge.

I am me with no desire to be they.
They have led me to nowhere and there I shall stay.
I shall never miss they blocking the view of every magical day.
I shall never be bothered by what they have to say.
I am me and I shall go my own way.

If by chance I miss your glance.
Be so kind and offer another chance.
My heart is pure but my mind is happen-stance.
I hear the music but only learning to dance.

We have learned the past's lessons sent
When the past is not part of our present

In the distance I could see the light
But every arrival brought the dark of night.
Again, and again the light would tease
And whisper a longing upon the breeze.

It wasn't until I faced the breeze and dark of night

Was I able to dismiss the dark and understand the light

Remained always behind me as I journeyed life's stormy seas

And illuminated my past as path of keys.

I find that love doesn't always rhyme

Sometime its sails are torn and tattered

It serves no purpose to defend or define

When its people in time fail at carrying it

It comes with no promise of time or distance

And will always be moments just happy to be

So, don't hold on to it's all you've ever known

And allow the gift's potential to set you free

In silence things work out in all imaginable ways

Very little can be offered in anything further to say

Customer service has little to do with right and wrong
But belittle to do with dance and song.

From a distance we see and hear.
In this distance wilt the seeds of fear
Or perhaps blossom the seeds of cheer
But neither shall reveal truths so dear
Until interaction brings our senses clear

In the leaves of Fall I see her face.
Not clearly defined but enough her outline I can trace.
Always one eye with lashes of lace.
And pouted lips that beckon embrace.
It's said we see what we look for in time and space.
But maybe we see what wishes us to give chase.
It's with that thought my soul should race.
As each leaf of fall searches for its destined place.

Beneath the belief of independence

Lay the silent truth of interdependence

Many might believe they're strong and alone

But constant acts of connection they condone

A butterfly's flutter changes the air we breathe

As a single thought can change everything we believe

Though the trend is to post our strife

I acknowledge they all might change our life.

As the leaves fly and flutter like a butterfly to the ground
They remind me of memories as they form a colorful mound
Making room for new memories or leaves reaching to the sun
But the journey of those that have fallen is far from done
As they become part of the tree's from whence they grew
Just like your memories will always be a part of you

Words can never be taken back or changed by utilizing the same hypocrisy with which they were said, written, or shared. Action is the only way to achieve redemption, and even then, they are not forgotten but merely forgiven. Perhaps we should be more concerned by our own actions in preface to the words we speak. The only people who know everything are those that have stopped learning and evolving for surely, they know everything they will ever know.

A bit too early I suppose

To witness nature, change its pose

But I still enjoy the fading to yellow

And bursts of rust add to the mellow

Even though true potential is concealed

The power of color will soon be revealed

And dance upon the chilled wind

In celebration of the newest end

Or perhaps it's not about the ending

But the gifts offered in a new beginning

Opportunities come and go like a moving train.

They are not looking for you in the sunshine or in the rain.

If you want them you must give chase and jump to escape the mundane.

Commit to finding our inner hobo to entertain.

And the world will become yours to retain

Waiting for reward or redemption from all your yesterdays

Will do nothing but diminish all your todays

And deny any new hope in your tomorrows.

It's ok to not be your old self

As life can be unfair and insane

Emotions are not meant to be put on a shelf

But used to accept that we will never be the same

An old man telling tales of once upon a time

All the while using his hands like a street mime

Once he ran to love but only found ultimate doom

Learning wants don't dictate if and when flowers bloom

Once he accepted love but it came down to having the wrong key

Learning people will be themselves regardless of how we see them to be

Once he decided to just be love and let life rhythm and rhyme

Learning love given is life's most soulful purpose upon time

I could hear her coming on her new bike

She was so proud of that brand-new trike

Whenever I heard that squeaky wheel

I sprang to the door to share her love so real

Every time she would wave and smile

Then turn in my drive and sit for a while

Until I would step out so she could tell me of her day

Then off she would go toward home, one house away

One day I heard the squeaky wheel and I rushed to her side

And I gave a little squirt of oil to her shiny red ride

Days went by and I could no longer hear her coming by

And sometimes by chance all I could do was wave goodbye

I waited on my porch what seemed forever for her to return

But return she did and seemed even more excited in turn

With permission I attached the cutest little red bell

And told her as long as the bell was ringing I knew all was well

But I think she knew the real reason for the gift
But never let on and just continued my life to lift
The broken is not always seeking your repair
Just your trust in the universe to relieve your despair

The wind ever so lightly blows
As if to be looking for a place to go
The moment of sunrise or sunset is hard to know
As both display such an ominous glow
Imagine the moon patiently in stow
For its turn to be a glorious show
The miracle of birth we may know
But tragedy of death brings us low
Appreciation of sacrifice we show
For opportunity upon us they bestow
In this season our consciousness will grow
Enlightened to the miracles we know
Imagine the miracles life will bestow
If always in this spirit we should go
And share the gift all life thru.

I was heading home from work as usual, and often I like to take a different route just to say I went somewhere I have never been or seen something I have never seen. I found myself on a narrow street in a neighborhood of very old, yet beautiful homes. Quickly I realized I may have made a mistake when I came upon a line of traffic and it was filling in behind me steadily. I couldn't see what the problem was but I suppose some sort of accident. I stayed in the line moving a couple inches at a time for what seemed forever. I decided I would just park and wait it out. I could watch the sunset through the trees and just enjoy the peace and quiet. I pulled into a space along the curb which happened to be in front of one of those old creepy but beautiful houses. It did not look like anyone even lived there anymore. It was warm and my windows were down and I was bouncing from my cellphone to the sunset. I was a bit startled when a voice appeared from the silence. It was a woman who appeared to be sweeping the steps of the house with a very odd-looking broom. She called out to ask me if I were lost. I assured I wasn't but merely waiting out the traffic backup. I asked her if she owned the house and she laughed and said "No, but I do know my way around it. Would u like a tour?" I glanced back at the line of cars and said "Sure, I would love to". She led the way into the door as I followed her but as I just the door and turned around she was gone. I looked around for her, as well as taking in how warm and inviting the place was. It did not look like the outside gave the impression that it would. I walked around until I came to a large staircase. I made my way up the stairs and I heard a door open at the end of the hall. As I approached the door I saw that it was the woman that had led me. She had changed clothes, maybe that where she had been while I wander around. She was now wearing a very tight black velvet dress. It seemed to change colors as she moved around in the candle light. She had let her hair down and it hung to her waist in glorious black waves. She turned her back to me and went further into the room and I immediately followed as though the choice was made by someone or something other than me. As I followed it became clear that this was a bedroom. She stopped and leaned back on a huge bedpost that went to the ceiling. She just stood silent looking back at me with dark eyes. When it became uncomfortable I asked her in a jovial tone "Are you flirting with me or just teasing?" Slowly she moved toward me. Her scent became alluring as she ever so gently brushed the cheek of my face with hers. Her breath tingled with magic as she softly whispered in my ear "I fully intend to do both. The question is to which will action grow within you?" as she stepped back it was though I was unable to move but

I did take notice of how the velvet on her dress was ruffled where she had pressed against me and where my hands lay upon her waist. She looked at her dress as if I drew her attention to it and the returned looking deep within my eyes as if waiting and I.

I was awakened but the sunlight upon my face. I looked around as I found myself sitting on red velvet loveseat and I was alone. It was the sunrise shining upon me. I made my way down the staircase and noticed how the house looked so much different in the light of day. The spider webs were everywhere and I don't know how I didn't notice them before. Just as I reached the front door I caught a glimpse of someone and I immediately thought it must be her. But to my disappointment it was just a mirror reflecting a portrait on the wall of a beautiful woman with long dark hair, in a black velvet dress, with eyes dark and deep, with almost the hint of a smile on her face. As I got to my car the sunrise cast a shadow of the house and it was just short of my car. It felt like a sign as to mean now or never so I.

To always accept an excuse is to always accept the regret.

Day by day we build our past
While our future never seems to last

He who ponders the if's and then's
Loses sight of the what's and when's

If and when will always end up being a very long wait.
Every moment should be treated like the first one out of the gate.

One cannot define or explain
A tortured soul's hidden pain
The scars lay silent in observation
Yet show profoundly upon reflection
But in reflection lay the goal
To touch the scars and soothe the soul
I love the blue between Day and Night
As Day holds on with all its might
Until the Night casts shadows that hark
And wait as the Day runs from the dark

I want to live my life in a place so high
That I get the first and last look at the sky
I want to always believe love is worth it
And never create reasons to regret it
I want to always seek Peace in all things

And relish in the quiet moments that brings
I want my soul to always be true and free
And never submit to what society says I should be
I want to forever remain humble and kind
Even if it's hidden within the secrets of me you find
I want to cherish every moment as my journey travels on
And always carry hope within and just Dream On

I get lost in the clouds and hear their confusion
They search for their dreams among the illusion
Some dark and grey and some bright and white
Yet they accept each other with no sign of fight
Sun and sky light the moments upon our eyes
And give some meaning to all of life's why's
As they change and evolve on their journey on
Their dreams seem to be merely to drift on

Time may heal but shall never erase
Any of the things we once had to face
And the others whom continue to embrace
To move past them is no disgrace
For in the mirror we seek our own face
Not just our position in life's race
Shadows of everything loom

With the approach of pending doom
As the sky loses its light
Until finally everything is lost from sight
Is anything still there if we can't see it
Was it ever there if we can't relive it
I imagine a place of quiet and peace
Gone but relived so as to never cease
Life seems to be a collection of things gone
We carry with us into a new dawn

A man traveling said his greatest fear was to be lost
A traveling man said his greatest fear was to not become lost
One might perceive the first as he who will follow
And the second as he whom we all yearn to follow
Be cautious how you perceive the lines you see
As how you choose will define the person you shall be
Things go by so much faster in the back seat
With no preview, choice, or gps time to beat
Nothing more than along for the ride
Or perhaps just accepting life in stride
But in silence I dream of more
And a front seat for the world to explore
I often must be reminded by my inner voice
That life is what we choose to accept as our choice

Relentless tears from skies cloudy and dark
On we fight but futile is each passing mark
Then suddenly time screams upon the night
Showing once more a tearless display of sight
It is not the marks of those tears wiped away
But those untouched that have the most to say

Take care with the circle you try to keep
That allows a negative in too deep
Being all connected is so very true
But that does not mean all get through
It is not the size that makes a star shine bright
But what is within that feeds the light

The sky is singing a song the wind can't hear
Yet the wind brings music to the sky sonneteer
But my favorite song throughout the year
Is when the sun's warm emotions become so clear
The beauty of life is not of journey or acquisition
But in the silent moments in between of our personal transition
But it is only when we draw near that allusion of destination
Do we encounter the truth forever hidden in silent recollection

From my soul emanates the music of my life
Some may soothe but some cut like a knife
New genres arise but it is the old that stir my soul
Even though living in the past has never been my goal
But I look into the past for a faint melody following along
Never will I hear it as I have not lived the life of a love song

Who we were is as much a part of whom today we see
As who we are is part of whom tomorrow we shall be
Those we fear would not accept certain parts of our past
Do not deserve to know who we have become at last
But the silent pretense we accept and carry inside
And the person we deserve to be will never coincide

The wind blows through the fences of life
That we see as our defense against strife
But it doesn't protect against feelings that flow
And cause the stirring of our soul to grow
Look for fences and that is all you will ever see

Seek not accountability from reactions
See the responsibility that lay in the actions

How often do we struggle to find the words we want to hear?
How seldom do we speak those words upon a listening ear?
We search for thoughts we can feel so we can make a post.
Then we deny or dismiss the thoughts that touched us the most.
There is no shame in speaking true in what you wish to hear.
And the only thing we have to lose in the end is the fear.
The fear of what others may think of thoughts that within you grew.
As the most important thing is the listening ear that is you.

One day I stopped and turned completely around
and stared at the view.
The first thing I noticed, to my dismay, was that all of the
doors were blue.
Some were weathered and worn, and some looked like
brand new.
I tried a few and found them locked and as for the rest,
I just knew.
Each door had a peephole but It was not meant to be seen
through.
But as darkness approached the light from within became
a visible hue.
As if we weren't meant to see beyond each door we had
once stepped through.

But the light from beyond would always enlighten each
step of our journey anew.
So, stop wasting precious time debating the right door and
put your trust in the blue
And forever more let it cast the light upon your journey to
the best you.

Every day we chase away the howls of the night that loom.
Every night we wander in search of those ghosts of doom.
It is not deeper into the darkness that we wish to go.
It is the search for the scent of a life we used to know.
Perhaps one day we will find the scent to call our own.
But until then the wolf within will continue to roam.

Achievements fade quickly and become lost in the sands of time
Mistakes remain a constant source of judgement for a lifetime
A sad world it is that derives a focus only on those things negative
And only striving for what we can get instead of what we can give
So, in the end we may reflect upon an unfulfilling life of compilation
And realize too late our mistake that life is soulfully about contribution

Eerie and profound is the sound of the flickering candle
upon the night
When artificial magic abandons and leaves us alone with
our own light
The light of our candle of life of which we only get one
chance to see
At first, we carry it high in our hand with anticipation of
what is to be
In time as it burns down we set our candle down as if to
pain we abide
In this light, we shall see behind and beside as clearly as
forward we stride
Lucky, is he who understands the chance to light another so
they can see
And show appreciation to others whose light helps us be all
we can be
For the lesson is not in the achievement of a light more
bright
But in the sound and sight found in the warmness of our
light

Release me from this pretentious affair.
To a life untrue beyond the despair.
In time is a lie without even a care.
And bears no fruit to the contraire.
To leave the crowd creates a path so bare.
But a path true to me I would gladly stare.

To look forward to the end.
Is to have nothing left to transcend.
To begin again holds no desire.
For fear the same forces shall conspire.
But there is solace in having tried.
And never again realize the universe lied.

A hidden truth hard to comprehend
Is upon another you should never depend
You will spend your life in doubt and dismay
Tears of regret will wash your dreams away
Suffer in silence those who fear rejection
As they meet every risk with objection
Committed to the belief of their perception
With no awareness of the preconception

Yet the fear they avoid by their election
Is given more than received upon reflection

In the wake of new beginnings
Stir the ghosts of past misgivings
Moments of noise they wait and hide
In silence release a drowning tide
Resistance tells the same tale of grim
Silent hope is risking the swim

Every day we get closer to choosing
Loosening grip on thoughts of losing
We think we must have a plan
But freedom is the absence of sand
To those who ask what will you do
Our reply shall be whatever we choose to

I will always ensure the last word is yours
Because my goal is to help you achieve yours
Refusing to argue will always be my choice
As I know no one hears the words of a raised voice
I will say be safe, and have fun when you go out
Not because I don't care but so my trust you will never doubt
I will always want you to hold your hand

To hear the word's, you draw thinking I don't understand
I will work hard and long pushing us to be apart
But I will always return because that's where I leave my heart
I will without advice always the best listener I shall be
Because I know my silence helps you to truly see.
I will not always say the beautiful things you need to hear
But I will write my emotions clear if you will just come near
As part of a team I will always do only my share
As I never want you to feel I don't depend on you to care
I am quiet, a thinker and will sometimes seem lost at sea
Never because of you, but how I was designed to achieve the best me
I will sometimes give the appearance of being so sad
But in sadness I'm better able to see all the reasons to be glad
I will never stop trying to win over your heart
And hope you will not let my need for reassurance tear us apart
But most of all I will always do my best to do and be all that is good
And trust the universe to show that I am merely a man misunderstood

On what basis do you demand
Compliance to all you command
Ownership and agreement to pay
Only refers to time out of my day
I follow my heart regardless the rule
With no desire to be someone's fool

My mind is mine alone to yield
Not just an asset for you wield
I will always be giving my all
Despite how you see the chips fall

We all have stories of why our heart might bleed
Some we tell but others we await another to read
Some will advise how you should lead your life
While others will merely compare to their own strife
Hope remains for who won't tell what to feel or do
But from the silence whispers "I am broken too"

Like the moon does seek and hide
As it runs from tide to tide
It yearns the touch of attentive hands
But can never shift from needing sands
Chased always away by light of day
Truth be revealed it can never stay
From me look away and do not see
As worthy I shall never be

Like a flower we inhale with affection
Some are led astray by attention

Like bouquets we create with ablation
Some are led astray by intention
But like the flowers left to abstention
Some will find peace in the accession

You can stare beyond all of your life
Take solace in the view through sorrow and strife
But until beyond landing you commit to fly
Your soul will eventually wither and die
But even a moment beyond dreams we realize
Can overcome the life of regret we visualize

She came to visit and stay one summer with friends
Her presence in my world surely did change the trends
She was another welcomed player of sports in the field
And like her swing, my heart she did freely wield
Her hippy van, to quote the time, was oh so keen
As we spent the day at the swimming hole so green
It was in the sunsets I found times special to my heart
We found ourselves alone with no one keeping us apart
Walking and talking we shared our emotional load
At a time, acceptable to walk in the middle of the road
Once we reached the bridge we sat close on the rail
And in silence enjoyed the breeze as the clouds sailed

We would cast pebbles into the trickling stream
And with each cast wonder silently of the others wish or dream
I would walk her home, but not to her drive but up the hill
And once there I would be overcome by a tender chill
It was just a hug but I never wanted it to come to an end
But upon release, down the hill again did I descend
The last time down that hill my heart would eternally burn
As I knew the moments were gone and she would never return
But as memories fade and disappear in time from my fragile mind
The feelings shall always be secured in the heartfelt ties that bind

Be it good and bad how time does fly
But one thing for sure, it shall never lie
It may lead us from astray to found
And always helping our feet hit the ground
It is when things do not go according to plan
I recall the dreaming boy within the man

The longer you wait to do the right things
The more likely it will be perceived as the wrong things
Yet the sooner you choose to do the right things
The more likely it will challenge you as being the wrong things

Proving that one should never reach beyond the span of
their own wings

I am not ashamed of how her name I can always hear
Whispered upon the breeze of every breath I hold dear
I make no apology for how the slightest touch of her skin
Turns my thoughts from mesmerized to chapters of sin
I make no excuse for the need to forever hear her voice
Sigh and moan with the reassurance that I am her choice
I have no regrets of giving myself up to within her be lost
I will never let go the taste and the passion of her lips
And how deeply from the entirety of my soul she sips
Fear has no choice but to relinquish any hold upon my voice
as I cast my breath of life singing the song of a girl named

It was a Wednesday, the day I broke away
From all the filters between me and life
So tired of others investments, left for me to pay
And the condemnation to remain within others strife
I leave care and concern for society's rules to play
And won't miss depending on those who carry the knife
My life is my own now, where ever I choose to carry it away
And to know no matter hill or valley peace will be rife

Beautiful days can cloudy and blue
Even when the gray should ensue
Perhaps a fool, but I so enjoy the part
Where all things appear to me as art
Beauty might be the artist's conviction
But beautiful is the depth of reflection

When we let the darkest shadows to fall behind
We lose the perception of all things as unkind
When we turn away from the walls we build
We lose belief that walls are cages of no yield
When we let go the need of down we must look
We lose the thought that finished is our book
Ups and downs are only parts that life will host
Sometimes it's the losses that mean the most

What does it take to realize a dream
Working hard is nothing but a scheme
It doesn't take money to see a sunset sky
And money can't find lost time gone by
Looking for the reward at the end of day
Remains futile at the least, to say
Your mind will remind that it is too late
But your heart can't be torn from the gate

Responsibility is something we have to do
Questioning whom to be responsible to
There is no end to escape the norm
Forever on a life of regret or reform

Maybe It is just a passing glance
A moment lost in a passing chance
Into the eyes a soul we might seek
Only to let fear quickly make us weak
And turn us away in a matter of a blink
The heart scolds the mind, shades of pink
And we return to the safety of hiding away
Until again the heart can keep the mind at bay
And seize a moment of chance at the gate
To see the true depths of perhaps a soulmate

Leave me alone in the silence
Unless you can hear the sound
Leave me alone with my thoughts
Unless what you offer will expound
Leave me alone on my journey
Unless you can see lost as found
Leave me alone with my emotions
Unless what you offer is profound

Leave me alone in the darkness
Unless you light dimly my background
Leave me alone to the future of me
Unless your soul can bring unbound

Does the setting sun ever lose the desire
To fill the remaining sky passionately on fire
Or maybe that desire does not come from sky
But a reflection of fire burning in the mind's eye
Tended by our soul, waiting for us to believe
All things are possible if positively we perceive

This road is only mine to travel alone
Experience in turns does my skill hone
Beyond shadow and storm, I will fight
With the vision of light within my sight
Choices made, never defined by doubt
Accepting change, life gives the route

Beyond the beautiful of every day
We toil over the lost time for pay
Those who see beauty on their own
When time comes, seeds of life are sown

Life may always control our borrowed time
But has no say over the moments in time

My life has been a journey of rejection
Rejection of a heart and soul well hidden
Hidden in the shadows by lack of belief
Belief held silent in fear of others thoughts
Thoughts forever lost in the unheard, waiting
Waiting alone with my unrealized dreams
Dreams I thought could hear my inner screams
Screams I have never had trust in them to fly
Fly I will now beyond the scars of rejection
Rejection I have found that only lives within
Within I will find my trust another door down
Down again by forces outside I will never find
Find me now in the colors of a sunset sky I fly
Fly with me as I am or for your loss I will not cry

Trust is nothing more than just words we say
Never is it given away without a price to pay
Loyalty is just a feeling we believe is shared
Until discovering we are the only one that cared
Trust in ourselves is something we should revive
So that in all things we will know we can survive

Loyalty is something in ourselves we should see
And never lose sight of the soul we are meant to be

Smothering it can be, the heat of day to day
Figuratively following the light, as they say
Waiting at red only intensifies the dread
To remain distant from where our soul is lead
Relief is only found when we can freely fly
Without the burden of light, except a sunset sky
It is in these moments my soul does soar
Leading my mind always in need of more
Like the scars that ensure a ride safeguarded
So too is my heart never left unguarded
Ride on I will, forever searching into the light
For illusion and fantasy my heart won't fight

There are those days our spirit, life does claim
And we seek something or someone to blame
But no matter the results will always be the same
Until you take your turn in changing the game

Purpose can change as new urges dawn
To simply be nothing more than gone
It didn't spiral out of control in one day
But slowly did as center changed to sway
Reaching too far it discovered the end
A place from which it could never mend
Dreaming of a star that shined so bright
And traveled so far sharing its light
The beginning of a journey to make a mark
I have never been a stranger to the dark
Something precious blows in a cool morning breeze
That soothes our soul and puts our mind at ease
It carries us through most of our day
Despite the roles we feel we must play
Peace becomes lost with the interaction
With those who's humanity is a poor reflection
Sad perhaps is a life lived unseen
Precious is a life lived for the moments in between

Take the chance for your heart to connect
Remain unseen, shielding the heart from neglect
Take the risk of something else to do
Remain still, settling for the loss of you
Take the offer and move into something more

Remain comfortable behind the closed door
Take the direction of your inner dreams
Remain without hope for more than it seems
Take the time to make your own list
Remain forever where only darkness exists

Moments of true silence are quietly profound
Yet life unattended will drown out their sound
Costumed distractions demand what we do
Without and regard to what's best for you
Following alone the empty promise of reward
Left with nothing but the regret of a coward
So, steal the moments where within you hide
And follow your heart and not false pride

Time can leave us tattered and torn
Hidden away within the loss we mourn
With the past held tightly in our hand
Giving no thought to the passing sand
A past held tightly will continue to deceive
Until time itself can the truth perceive
The notes of life are best left to unfold
Making room for life's miracles yet untold
Writing on the wall is never clear

Despite it being all, I ever hear
Screaming over the voice of inner fear
Yet in silence I drift upon life, unable to steer
Someday I will choose the writing to hold dear
And the wall will fall, crushing the fear

Beyond the horizon of hopes and dreams
The sky is forever blue as the sun gleams
A sunset conveys no more than a doubter perceives
To receive more is to hope and believe
Cast your thoughts beyond the sunset sky
And the dreams of your soul will never lie

I search beyond the grey for something new
My mind holds grey yet my soul seeks blue
Call it a belief or see it as a clue
Beyond the grey will always be blue
Trust is hard but trust we should our souls view
And derive your own meaning of all is blue

I ponder a point from which no return
Where life is more than a heart to burn
A journey so far away from you as a joke
And never again wait for who next will poke
Into a silence where a phoenix may rise
And fly beyond a tortured soul's cries

It is with surprise our eyes do meet
Be it just for a moment it resigns bittersweet
The first time her soul met mine she was alone
But every time since, I noted a chaperone
Inner conflict rages with thoughts of missed chances
Despite the beaconing I feel from her glances
Behind my disguise upon her exit I cordially speak
I can feel her tremble with thoughts I long to seek
Our paths uncross and my soul fades blue
Dreaming of the next chance anew
To know her with the butterfly tattoo

Trust is nothing more than just words we say
Never is it given away without a price to pay
Loyalty is just a feeling we believe is shared
Until discovering we are the only one that cared
Trust in ourselves is something we should revive
So that in all things we will know we can survive
Loyalty is something in ourselves we should see
Never losing sight of the soul we are meant to be

Origins awaken with no concept of constraint
Constraint is built over time of fear and doubt
Doubt you will or doubt you won't we create
Create a place from which we fight to escape
Escape only exists within the limits of the mind
Mind sight captively unable the truth to see
See within and unto you will appear the key
Key to paradox lay in the building a bigger box

The path is narrow and the air is always thin
Time is on borrow as the same day comes again
Limited is view other than past or expectation
The sky is never blue except within perception
Beyond the path lay truth of the depths to haunt
Beaconing the risk of proof in its silent taunt

I find no joy within the day to day
I find no truth to they say it will come
I find no answers from within defined
I find no evolution in my heart refined
I find no comfort in another's demise
I find no trust beneath everyone’s lies
I find no love in the emotionless sighs
I find no hope outside the silent cries
I find exactly what deeply I may seek
I find a strength not meant for meek
I find desires unknown by the weak
I find myself when within I dare peek

Every sunset I see is a welcoming rave
For the coming of the darkness I crave
Bringing balance to the world of sight
Shading all things visible in the same light
The mirror of shadows obscures the fear
To release my soul's voice for all to hear
But only until once again comes the light
As my soul fades into the silence of sight

Afar had he swum from off that bridge he did jump
And chose to drown waiting for life his lungs to pump
But one day he heard his mind say it was okay to go home
The threats no longer present that forced him to roam
But just beyond that perceived point of no return
His mind recalled images that made his scars burn
But into the fire was the only relief, for long he sought
Ablaze he ventured back carrying but a single thought
And between deaf ears and deceitful lips pulled the trigger
Only to be awakened in pain and in a state of rigor
He cursed his mind for once again tearing him apart
As he had forgotten there is no safety for a trusting heart

Silent is the journey deeper and deeper into the age of night
Night we unknowingly settle for in the absence
of our own light
Light from within allowing in all things
to see the opportunities
Opportunities hidden from the conditioned mind that is life
Life being unrealized except beyond the shadows
of death and youth
Youth being the gift of light born to be carried
through life eternal

Life is poetry, perceived today yet realized over time
Following its own unique rules for reason and rhyme
We often force the progression and take all the credit
Only to be humbled by life forcing its corrective edit
Poetry is life, written in the words and thoughts known
Trusting the poetry of life to carry us beyond the unknown

Afar he had swum from off that bridge he did jump
And chose to drown waiting for life his lungs to pump
But one day he heard his mind say it was okay to go home
The threats no longer present that forced him to roam
But just beyond that perceived point of no return
His mind recalled images that made his scars burn
But into the fire was the only relief, for long he sought
Ablaze he ventured back carrying but a single thought
And between deaf ears and deceitful lips pulled the trigger
Only to be awakened in pain and in a state of rigor
He cursed his mind for once again tearing him apart
As he had forgotten there is no safety for a trusting heart

The air is crisp and feels of hope
The breeze brings strength to cope
Through my soul it pushes away the past
Leaving enhanced those things meant to last
The struggle to focus on work is very real
As my soul wants the choice of what to feel
So, inside this box I go for the wasted day
And time itself is the ultimate price to pay

If a blue sky can sprinkle with rain
What more is there we might attain
Sun in my eyes and rain on my face
Drawing my soul away from the race
Perceptions as varied as they may be
I choose the view of dreams I can see

With every smile into my eyes you stare
Opens my heart in places that have forgotten to care
Dreams begin by running my fingers through your hair
The touch of your hand upon places I lay bare
Drawing me to touch your skin so soft and fair
Consuming my soul with your aroma of love and despair
And teasing my heart with lust open to share
To give and receive leaving nothing to spare
But awakened from a dream as you pass by me unaware
Leaving nothing of you but a wish to only dare

My passion for the wind came early on
A child behind dad on the bike I eagerly got on
Quickly I learned holding on tight was a must
But more than that I learned about trust
Sometimes I had to get off to cross a stream
Which taught me how to be part of a team
Sometimes we would go down and hit the ground
And lay there and laugh and listen to how silence would sound
Every adventure began and ended in an obstacle to overcome
As across the fronts a ditch was dug as a warning of unwelcome
He always reminded me to hold on and into the wind we would fly
Across that ditch to the other side dismissing its unwelcome cry
I carry those lessons still when facing life's ditches
Throttle her rich and fly over those bitches

Into the wind is where are lost many hats
Hats we wear to disguise what lay hidden
Hidden away waiting to again be discovered
Discovered in the naked and raw state of truth
Truth hidden in the pretentious cover of the book
Book that risks being read into rejection

No clouds, no crowds, just empty space
Space just enough to let loose wildest dreams
Dreams of come true and hopeless to pursue
Pursue and ensue forever echoing in the silence
Silence of a soul trusting only of being lost
Lost, of the chase for only make believe

If a living could be made from thoughts I share
How quickly I would trade for being seen as rare
Even if difference it made to one who may care
Deeds pass and fade and upon a soul does wear
Intentions be laid but in success never to share
Debts remain unpaid except in disappointment stare

He was sorry for working himself to your death
Regretful for not giving beyond his last breath
It was you always unsupportive of choosing
Yet always demanding the conflict of playing without losing
Commitment is sold like strings for shoes
Not a perception of choice free to abuse
The was in sorry changes to is from the pain
Sorry for his blindness to the drowning rain
Is it passion when we raise our voice
Or sounds of silence in which we rejoice

Is passion born with us like love to a lover
Or is life the passion chosen by a mother
Is passion derived from that we do for a living
Or is it more about what we find joy in giving
Is passion something we must endure in strive
Or is it ever changing like the seasons of life
Is passion just an act of choosing a choice
Or is it a passion to be led by our Soul's choice

Dreams are the way the mind likes to play
Unwritten stories of yesterday and someday
Little do they have to say related to today
The price we pay not to trust what they say
Believing does lay secrets of finding our way
As dreams come your way by actions of today

Regret of past day is to waste a lesson of today
Today to live is to move away from yesterday
Yesterday flags of white lay silent in the wind
Wind that waits for us each our own sails to fill
Fill they will but only with courage our own life to fulfill
Fear for tomorrow is fought in the actions of today
Today is not the result of your past and future
Future and past are the result of your today

Today is the now weakness waits in surrender
Surrender is a way in which we choose to stay
Stay your own mast by getting off your ass

From the demise of every today's sunrise
I find the sight tinted the color of insight
I dare not the day waste in life's eternal haste
To pursue the choice of the soul's inner voice
For he who waits and with regret debates
Frets and longs for a path he already belongs
When a sunrise is gone it continues to move on
With passion of debt to the dream of a sunset
When shadows are falling it continues the calling
Consouling cries on the path to today's sunrise
Into the wind I ride no longer my soul so shy
The clouds align as pyramids under a blue sky
The sun comes close to paint upon bended knee
Beckoning my pause to seek more than I see
As I sit under this sun on a bench in a park
My wonderment explodes of things kept dark
Why is it easy to ride away with nowhere to go
Perhaps a key to life is to trust and not know

Bound by the task to explain whence we came
Becomes an encircling path of regret and blame
To believe that who we are we must convince
And ignorance of life's lessons is no coincidence
Our journey is a game of repetition and chance
Meant to teach lessons of escape to advance

There are those who always try to be kind
But even they have thoughts of never mind
In soft voices, it is hard to hear what they hide
In their silence where the thoughts do collide
And battles are fought over the inner blindness
That allows the harshest neglect of self-kindness

A silent walk at sunrise
Urging the silence within my soul to rise
The journey is taken to no particular place
Except where I can feel the sun on my face
The chatter of chaos upon the wind is faint
But the sounds of life know no restraint
The trickling sound of water around me
Grow stronger in repetitive moans of an ocean beyond me
Scampering feet of birds on the edge of a gutter
Transforming into a sight of wings all a flutter

Onward I go to perhaps hear so far away
I no longer care for back to see my way

I cannot follow your path or seek your shore
Again, setting adrift all my heart has in store
If by chance our paths under stars shall cross
In a moment of eternity to the wind to toss
Entirely invested in the moment at hand
Beyond any concern for the shifting sand
Into the storm of life my heart to throttle
I cast my soul's message within a bottle

The most daring thing I have ever done
Is to dream a dream but continue to run
Poetry is art and in art lays expression
What better way to escape depression
To use one's thoughts as a shield of armor
But in those words, lay my shield of honor
Let come what may in an existence alone
Find strength in expression exceeding unknown

Starting the day under a sky cloudy and grey
And the green of life hinting at fading away
Like moods our seasons fight for change

Reluctant to choose in the heart and soul exchange
But in our fall, is where our choice is revealed
In perception of color bursting from within concealed

I WISH I HAD THE TIME

to stand by and watch the world burn
to be okay living on what I didn't earn
to be a father defined by nine to five's
to be what I am not to mothers-wives
to not worry about working for my pay
to not worry about providing a way
to take me time without words of neglect
to avoid a life of constant vivisect
to participate in things, I am selfishly absent
to live a life worthy of blessing and assent

Face the rain and feel it soothe your pain
Confront the sun and dry the tears that run
Release to the moon your fear and find a listening ear
Face what you must confront to release your soul beyond
the storm front

In her presence, he could only think to hold his breath
As a testament to a conviction greater than death
In her eyes, an attraction from which he dared not look away

For fear of implying her soul was not reason enough to stay
In her face, a story telling of living beautiful but intricate as lace
But just enough shadow and unknown calling him to the chase
In her hair, so soft his fingers entwined as though he was blind
Searching for the knots and tangles of life his purpose to unwind
In her skin, aged but supple and sweet like the choicest of fine wines
Hoping to sip upon like the best books seeking pause at the best lines
In her soul, he sees a place he imagines of trust and passion with doors open wide
As patiently he awaits the sound of a voice whose tone beckons him to come inside

We think our walls are high but paths cut deep
Souls howl beckoning cries trusting walls to keep
Like ink on a page dries the words choice to leap
Dissuading any who tries with darkness they reap
But in the sound of cries not our own we truly weep
Confusing a walls size for a soul's cut with blood that seeps
Awakening with surprise within the secrets we keep
Those who hear our cries can heal our scars walls so steep

Too late for me as the course of challenge has run
The only challenge left to me is to live under the sun
Finding peace within the spider web life has spun

Holding the good for me and everything else to shun
Leaving go societies implied need to prove or stun
Finding solace in shadows that always with me have run
I know it's our first date
and I've only just arrived at your gate
But I have a desire I must relate
with the courage of my beating heart rate
With a belief in fate
before time to judge and rate
Who we are before debate
using only the energy of now to relate
Before it's too late
Passions first appearance to celebrate
My intention to kiss you I state
to the you my soul did dilate

Tired of always needing to be, she just wanted to get away. Before she knew it, she was driving with no destination in mind other than the direction of a way to achieve. I was a beautiful yet crisp sunny day. The sun was warm upon her skin except when in shadow she drove on despite the chill seeking bone. It must have been a fall of season by the expanse of color broadened upon her horizon. Feeling as though she was doing well on the test she took leave at the sign road side rest. As if welcoming her alone the space was empty but for the exception of a single motorcycle of black. With a drink and a smoke, she wandered to a bench positioned for the setting sun. just beyond her circle she noticed the man in a leather vest also positioned for the view she would seek. He looked up from his phone and with his eyes acknowledged hers did he meet. The thoughts circled her and she chose the one that he was playing games by the way he typed intently focused. Turning away she took her seat and became part of the view and sounds so sweet. The smoke of her cigarette drifted and faded away along with her concern for who and where she was dealt to be. In the silent sound, she heard the click of a lighter from the soul behind her bound. As the light of the setting sun did change she noticed a scrap of paper beside her on the bench. Reluctantly opening the folds to find the beginnings of a poem written by someone before her on this bench she sat. after reading it over and over in search of its truth she folded it back and laid it back down. The sun had set and its color had gone so she arose on her unknown way she must go. The bike still remained the only other sign of life besides her in this park. As she shut her door and looked ahead the was walking toward her but sat down again upon her bench. Once again, he looked her way but it was too dark, despite the park lights, to see any message from his eyes. He picked up the scrap of paper on which was written the poetry she found and again returned to typing on his phone. She wondered if he or could he have in her approach sensed her need for the view he shared. Had he given up his seat and patiently waited for me to leave or did he leave a piece of his soul in hopes my judgement be swayed. Already forward on her road it would seem she would never know. By dark of the night she continued to drive alone. She was the only soul on the road for as far as she could see or imagine. Somewhere in the night came a light from behind. It grew larger and closer until alongside it vanished from her rear view. It was the man from the park on the bike of black thundering by in the darkness of the night. He paused by her side but gave no look or sign of intent. He pulled to in front where he matched her souls pace until she understood it was no game or race. He led her from the night into the new sunrise of sight. With the sun in her eyes she never noticed he was gone now, forever to dwell within her soul's insight.

Through the barrenness of life to carry a picture
on our walls
Walls, we don't look upon to see except to straighten
and dust
Dust that clings over time unseen until seen
by an outside light
Light of truth that reveals the pictures image
we protect and hide
Hide we must since the picture fell
and is obscured of shattered glass
Glass shatters so impossible to fully clean they become
part of our view
View from distance is maintained but up close
we step with caution
Caution we trust to guide us away from a dusting
past experience
Experience that defends against images that can cut deeply
Deeply we mourn the loss of a picture where closely
we fear walking
Walking the same path over until we place another picture
on the wall

I wish for things I will never possess
To find treasure on islands I would miss
should I have never question the abyss
the hand of kind with soft caress
the heart and mind free to express
the soul's intimate dance of recklessness
I wish for things I will never possess
To find treasure on islands I would miss
should I have never question the abyss
the reassuring touch of endless
the division between as seamless
the evolution of being witness
I wish for things I will never possess
To find treasure on islands I would miss
should I have never question the abyss
the give within forgiveness
the gentle within gentleness
the tender within tenderness

Life is one of the many gifts with subdued appreciation
Appreciation set aside by the tearing of gift wrap
and ribbons
Ribbons of length in some bows and cut short
in other reflective binds
Binds unseen until realized in life's tragic loss
Loss we feel with appreciation for the pain
Pain of loss is where we become alone with creation
Creation of blessed moments seen all at once
Once and forever we now carry the lost souls
Souls lost forever now living on through you
The heat was intense and begging for relief
Every breath taken is a moment forsaken
The steam mimics regret so slippery and wet
The sweat does burn with a fiery yearn
Times standing still does anticipation instill
Every action of recover to the prelude another
Skin is drenching to the point of flinching
To release this tension born unto this kitchen

Unto the clouds we cast our why's
Hoping for answers too our silent cries
Unto the moon we release all the lies
And start again in the light of a sunrise
Day by day we toil away counting the tries
Awaiting to be found by the path of the wise
An obvious truth we may never realize
The path we must seek it one that flies
With no lines or rules another may devise
In their lead bringing your soul's demise
So, before the ink of the story of you dries
Stand up and thrust your wings upon the skies

The clinched grip of grief will never offer relief
To await a change is to your life exchange
The fist you wear upon your shoulder you share
As in the mind so is the attraction in kind
The change for new comes in the change of you
But to find out one must cast away all doubt

The words we read are without power or creed
Until from them we conceive a path laced of seed
The writer is perceived a ghost of the spirit's need
Until within we listen to that which ghosts do feed
The reader is the ghost of silent needs to concede
Until the words stimulate the silence to succeed
Tragedy of the heart does not show for all to see
They lay hidden within the soul we have come to be
The heart carries on under the illusion of being free
Confused by the wanton need and desire a jailer's key
To a lock purposefully broken by the minds decree
Awaiting again a time when the heart and mind agree
That no longer shall they be their own worst enemy
And face risk as the soul they were meant to be

Lines are drawn from colors before a dawn
Rules are made by those knowing only shade
Earth of our own but never to truly own
Our own mind we yearn but lost in effort to earn
Honesty left in the sea of success to drown
But searched for in those of crown
Truth told only as to please or in effort to appease
The promise of youth is but sage centering the wisdom of age
The focus of love upon one limiting the emotional gift for everyone

Perfection is the goal set but only found in each and every sunset
I am but one of many whose name you won't find any
For that is a toll for the release of your soul
Time ends as a tie within questions of why
Amid the battle of regret to scream or cry
Hindsight's echo rages against an empty sky
So blue with fear of another truth to deny
Our spherical horizon taunts us to imply
More to see is found in the higher we fly

I hear you screaming but I have long since passed your street
I haven't the desire nor intention of turning back to your deceit
My release is complete with silence I cast upon the winds discreet
Leave my existence as nothing more than a plague of your conceit
The window was drawn merely in black and white
Yet the intention is meant of cheery and bright
So, when you find no window in sight
Search within and create your own light

Choose we will when presented with a choice
Choose we won't when we perceive no choice
Choose we can when internally we seek the choice
Choose we can't when externally we fear the choice
Choose we have when we fail to act upon the choice

Choose we haven't when actions don't reflect the choice
Choose not to remain and wait for you to make a choice
Choose to transcend the limitations we place on choice
Choose not to follow or obey the rules governing choice
Choose the pieces true of you and be the creator of choice

It is not for a reflection of what I see that I stare
It is the innocence to wonder what might be out there
It is beyond the boundaries of sight I wish to dare
It is the connection of reflection of all things do I care

Age is a number we abide by within the illusion of time
Time that has no beginning or end beyond the perceived
Perceived of limits to diminish the reality of truths unseen
Unseen as a life lived entirely in the mind in our dreams
Dreams we feel in the moments we let go of what things seem
Seem is to give up the choice to imagine love and life as real
Real are the moments we forever carry beyond age of experience
Experience we collect to build the being we shall be in the next stages

Stages that travel in the circle of life with no regard for an age timeline
Timeline that only exists within the believing mind without questions
Questions abound of why but few have the courage to ask why not
There is a story of a day when the moon took lunch around noon
He sat down in a park hoping none would recognize or bark
A little boy did so incline to join the moon taking an obvious shine
Plenty of what and why until the moon offered to share his pie
So, in the silent lull they ate until the boy and the moon were full
The moon questioned the boy to see who and what he wanted to be
I have never known who or what I shall be should I ever be grown
I trust your light to guide as I aspire to succeed in each step with pride
To myself I want always to be true even through the moments so blue
The sun was fading and it would be time soon for the serenading

To a told story's tune about how a boy became the man in the moon

Confrontations are never done by those being responsible
They are done by those who suffer the hand irresponsible
The longer it demands attention the more it takes advantage
Casting risk upon those an unwanted point of vantage
It becomes a tedious wait for a self-induced explosion
Only to suffer further antagonistic acts from the implosion
The point is reached when escape seems the only viable solution
And leave those responsible alone to reflect their lack of resolution

Dip the brush of the color that feels right
Watch the stroke fade from dark to light
Take notice the end is merely lines of sight
Guiding the hand from beneath dark of night
Be not afraid to dip again the brush with foresight
Or rinse away and change with the color hindsight
Life is a painting of which we own the copyright
Never completed nor subjected to wrong or right

Commonalities sought will fail to exist
When the truth of your soul you resist
Yet even in the path of truth you persist
A solidary soul will evolve as a defeatist
Unless the positive risk of heart you enlist

You can speak words for them never to be heard
You can share thoughts for them never to be understood
You can defend yourself for them to never give a damn
You can seek the source of hate for them to never change
You can bear the burden of guilt for them to insist upon more
You can walk away in silence for them to throw rocks behind you
You can raise your walls for them only to rain down upon you
You can change your view for them only to punish others because of you
You can end all that is you for them to never change in your eternal view
You can do nothing that will ever justify a fire for them to feed
You can wait for truth to breathe for them only to have no one to care

You can do nothing but move on, hardened from the game
for you not for them

The yellow lines were worn and fading away
Not much longer would they imply the way
Drifts of challenge leave them with little to say
Rejection is close at hand in the longing of some day
To journey beyond lines keeping rebellion at bay
And living for the moments found in today

Many are the things we hope to **change**
So much time **is** wasted on lists to arrange
For which nothing is ever **gained** in exchange
Except **in** the hope and sorrow interchange
The key perhaps is in the **choosing** any one thing
And **to** follow it until change it will no longer bring
Then choose another of **hope** over sorrow to sing

We search for the rhyme found in the lines of a spell
Cast upon the heavens and into the vowels of hell
For the eyes who understand the story ours will tell
And in their truth, comes strength of the lies to dispel
Finding but one soul from two, into forever to dwell

Beneath the beauty of what is lay the beauty of what could be
But we rest comfortably in the rhythm of a melancholy sea
Waiting on the moon's beckoning call to the tide a decree
For the waves upon our soul to draw back an allow us to see
But the moon will not hear the plea of a soul already free
Until we reach out with belief in the unrest of possibility

The lone strands of hair in her eyes caressing her face
The soft but textured brush behind the ear ending the chase
The willingness of touch sending chills and the heart to race
The sound of her breath as it passes her lips in silent embrace
The words unsaid but shared upon the skin within a trace
The dream dared and shared bringing about the souls unlace
The eternal moments that the notion of time does displace
The dream of these things holds on despite life's quest to erase

Sometimes, quite often, always, I question my own thoughts
Thoughts I sometimes wonder if they are my own possession
Possession, quite often, I fight for in the silence to hear the truth
Truth, always, I perceive uniquely from the depth of my soul
Soul I have trained to be both, my sword as well as my shield

Over and over again we set out, but never to follow thru
In letting go of all we know in search of what we knew
But all paths circle back to the vision dominantly held of you
A journey back will always reveal itself in our current view
But perhaps it is the minds window that offers the best clue
By closing the window and trust the view of a door anew

Silhouettes of orange and gold transform the green of old
The breath of life turns crisp and blows a whimsical wisp
The season emits the wisdom of letting go in order to grow
And giving of yourself back to be returned in times of lack
Outlines soon easy to trace but find soul lies deeper than a face
And the loyalty of life is found in the colors displayed in strife

There is no time beyond the now
On what to spend it I search for how
Time that shows of furrowed brow
Slips away to nothing but end to endow

Once in a while I could feel the sun light over my shoulder
Yet the breath of the wind grows colder and colder
Tears gently fall from the sky and drift on clouds that
smolder

In thoughts of what is and what could be through eyes of a beholder
In the time of space where thoughts we chase
Chase always we do the road's empty turns
Turns empty of traffic with no end in sight
Sight we feel a need in fear of stories untold
Untold being the story's unwritten fees
Fees untold by the roads red and green autumn trees
Trees of life offering only safety in choice

Ponder we must yesterday's regrets alive in today's sorrow
Escape we cannot todays obligations to tomorrow
Careless we act with the illusion of time we borrow
Dependent we stay to the vision of someday is always tomorrow

A sliver of a moons watchful eye over what remains of the sun in the sky
You hear no questions of how or why as the sun drifts upon a silent goodbye
Be it a day of cheer on high or tears to cry the bond is one unable to deny
The sacrifice and loyalty tie that binds them in the forever sky

The moon was at piece while the sun flailed color upon the sky in release

Beyond the sky I would stare and thoughts of peace it would share

Once from a place deep within afar came the vision of a shooting star

I hoped to watch it as far as I could see but it seemed to be seeking me

As the speed of its trail hastened like it was caught within a windy gale

Engulfed in the lights attraction it showed me a memory of life's connection

When the shooting star was me as a reminder of everything we can be

I spread my wings upon the shadows of night
Without any need to prove my flight in day light
I can soar anywhere my soul chooses to go
Without any desire to show my heart glow
I search for only the truth that underlies
Without any belief in a perception of lies

The waves of blue dance upon the shore of you
The caps of white accent the colors of life's insight
The stones at our base redirect the flow that we chase
As the tide of life draws breaths to reveal its depths

Anticlimactic is the race from love to hate
Regardless the pace of a tempestuous fate
There is no victory release of habits we create
Nor will the lies cease in the thoughts we miscreate
Alone are we to blame for the life we waste
Giving hate a name until it becomes an acquired taste

I watch the people come and go
Inspired by some I will never know
Tired of some that cling but never grow
Then I look to those I depend on to row
Imagining places, they will never allow me to go
One cannot go farther than the desire your circle will show
But it ultimately will be decided by the desire of you
To settle in or step beyond the limits and let them go

I never feel worthy of a sky painted blue
To humble to consider it my reflective view
Yet too proud to let go the emotions that ensue
Wasted days in search of what my heart holds true
Collected days of color my soul does imbue
But there is no combination in life for blue
Other than my choice of what to cling to

We find comfort in the sadness.
And dream to escape the madness.
Is the reason why we remain aware.
To remind us the darkness not to share.
Or to point the way out is inward sharing
And risk the darkness falling upon the caring

Success has always been the limit of another's intent
Waiting among those you are sent will end in the discovery your life is spent
Much you will blame and vent but still you continue to dwell a tragedy resident
The choice evolves as settling in decent or facing the fear of your ascent

As your soul, I always have to talk the heart off the cuff to
our sleeve.
Why are we led by the heart, so easily deceived?
With our wisdom, shouldn't the soul answer the door to
those we might receive?
It takes intent to search a soul yet the lack of intent causes
the heart to bleed.
I will be known as a breaker of rules to this game we
perceive.
We shall be offered soul and heart and eliminate the
confusion of what the heart may conceive.

Many lives have we lived into the over
And still we fear the starting over
Spending more of our time in the over
Than collecting our time in beginning over

Every sunrise of past tells a story of things that don't last
Sun on my face and squinted eyes held fast I am shown the
land of never last
Consumed by the reddish glow I hear the words of letting go
The warmth is consuming in the absence of assuming
As the illusion of time we sever we find a truer meaning of
forever

This sunrise is forever new and carries its light into
tomorrow anew

Dandelions will blow with seeds that they sow
The wind won't know where they might grow
Leaving some with the sorrow of just having to let go
If only with courage in tow they had the choice of where to go
And escape life's harrow and grow beyond the lines of shadow

If it were not for the gray giving it away
Clouds white and steady paused in the light
Stickers for you to place on a canvas of blue
Creating a sky upon which we dream to fly
In the spirit of free to choose how we see
In search of choices reflecting our inner voices

As I wait for the sun to set, I find myself in a place of debt.
I ensure I have no place to be or anything else I need to see.
Time passes relatively slow and at this speed magic steels
the show.
I forget who I am supposed to be and my thoughts reach
out for who I might be.
Things that matter become clear and precise while
everything else falls to my own devise.

My emotions pull hard against my restraints until
vanquished are any constraint.
A tear may ease down my cheek but it certainly is not a
reflection of bleak.
I feel no shame for expression in violation of the game but
emotional strength seeks no fame.
As the colors and contrast fill my skies, Peace becomes the
vision unto my eyes.

The mourning fog collects with a letting go of your pretense
The bumpy ride offers reflection on rougher times of our
defense.
We hear the warnings but we still react with all our sense
For life is truly but a play built around the thrill of suspense.
Once you can filter out all the silly nonsense

As I sit at these functions as a party of one
Surrounded by other families and loved ones
I search the past for what I have ever done
To deserve the lost chances and dreams undone

Amidst all the noise there is a silence beneath our voice
The one that is heard without speaking a word
It is here we hide our light in the open of plain sight
We do not envy those who must their colors disclose
But in reflection we feel better about the spectrum of color
within we conceal

The flowers that grow where-ever they may
Don't realize hidden emotions they convey
Alone upon the breeze of life do they sway
In search of giving of themselves they stay
Leaning away as admiration walks their way
In fear of what is taken in the walking away

The rain has finally subsided
The streets remain so crowded
Uniqueness is a freedom afforded
The light of the sky is forwarded
To the neon bright and illuminated
A world unique but variable created
Full of love and life encouraged
The vision of New York recorded

Of no greater addiction than the regret
Of those things we may or may not forget
Of dreams or time that we shall never beget
Of pending release from regrettable mindset

The lights grow dim and things go back the way they have been
But things are never quite so grim when what we learn grows within
And each time from the rim we dare step away we grow stronger again
Until the circle from which we stem is no longer a boundary holding us in
My broken heart will never be able to start again
But that's not to say it's not capable of love again
It may never again fall in wonder of what this is
But will stand tall from the fall, knowing what love is
It will whisper loyalty from its scars to a delicate touch
But it has learned to stay behind until the soul you touch

His path has been long and narrowing
And with each breath more harrowing
To the place he couldn't breathe at all
As closer and closer caved in the wall
The voices grew louder in his mind

Of the pending end did they remind
And with no shame urged him to run
Upon another path as this one is done

It was in a weak moment that I moved a wall and set my soul free
And now, even in moments of strength, it resists returning to me
I give chase but it's more like being dragged from place to place
Hoping I will stop resisting freedom and participate in its surprising pace
As it leads through the depths of emotion and the heights of miracles in sight
Searching for love in all things and peace even in the darkest of night
But I have learned to harbor no regret for the moments I've let my soul roam
Because from within the experience I have never felt more soulfully at home

Tormenting thoughts of what to do or where to hide
Are rarely resolved in things we push ourselves to decide
Life is not merely a box to open, close, dissect, or divide
It is an endless portrait of you from the colors you provide

Paint from your heart and fear not when colors clash or collide
Just accept it as part of your palate and the torment will subside

The risk you resist for fear of what you will owe
Will be the reward you might regret but never know
A debt of limited value upon yourself to bestow
Shall pale in comparison to the debt you owe to you

Beyond the boundaries of time and date
Roams the energy of fantasy and fate
A stranger of light upon the dark of night
A stranger to remain upon the illusion of sight
Whispers exchange in a silent need to seek
The introductory words denied to speak
But the chilling shadows offer no retraction
From the stranger known only as attraction

When the voices have nothing to say
Beyond the whispers of giving it away
This life so lucky, as some would say
Yet we yearn a change with every day
To match the evolution of our own way

Fear not of karma, upon you to prey
But have trust in the path of you to stay
Or the loss of you will be the price we pay

I will wait for you in the stars
From which the moon was born
A healing energy of time and scars
Uniting once and for all beyond lovelorn
Together beating as one from two pulsars
A light forever shall two souls adorn
I show you attention but you will not see
I stand beside you but you do not believe in me
In many ways I speak but you do not understand
My soul lingers always near you with no demand
In the breeze I whisper your name upon a deaf ear
But I always listen when into your soul you peer
The only hope I draw is when in fear you feel held tight
For it is I that holds you tight on this hallowed night

Torn covers and tattered pages worn thin
The book of you as written without a pen
We spend forever deciding where to begin
And then we review it over and over again
Though it is never written now as it was then

But the circle of life is much about the admin
And the lessons learned in ink to start again

The questions of self we cannot answer are few
Few that we seem to always answer I don't know
Know that we find fear in the multiple answers
Answers we refuse to choose one over another
Another or one both lead us away from the doorway
Doorway we hide from choice vulnerable to fate

Fate that may repeat our journey's way to this door
Door that may lead to the hope that lives in a dream

I used to seek the light when it was at its height
But now I see the greater light just beyond the night
It is easy to shine where darkness is not to be found
But it is from a darkness that light becomes profound
In the shadows, life has a greater message to show
Of a beautiful soul's fight in holding on or letting go

The moon draws our eyes into the night sky
But the greatest pull is when the moon is full
No matter what the state it feels it can relate

To the journey of man to become what we can
As it shares light but never disappears from sight
Together they match pace in a circle of life race
A pledge of trust taken, never to be forsaken
A story of love written in the sky above

I often stare upon the hourglass of time and wonder
Why we never notice more weight above than under
Or the gravity of the pending storm of crackling thunder
And the reflection against the sand causing a deep sonder
The moment of balance will be the cause of great discern
And away from the flowing sand we cast our concern
And look upon the glass itself for the message to learn
By cherishing each grain of moments, you will no longer
yearn

Life is not a book of you waiting to unfold
It is a book written continually of truths untold
You have no right to condemn the movie to comply
To a story that you make little effort yourself to apply
Nothing just falls easily upon your life as you want it
Unless you put forth the choice of effort to earn it
Success and setbacks are all part of the journey to you
Laying down the pen because of either is not the thing to do

To be free is not just to receive all you imagine or see
It is the freedom to pursue and choose how you want life to be

If you often feel the need yourself to promote
Refusal to move past the healing it may denote
Search within for the need to prove to who
And you shall find the only one fooled is you

My life is a search within the shadow of distraction
Blindly following an essence of light within attraction
As much as I try to chase what I believe a dream
Yet they never materialize to be what they might seem
But from the shadows that set my soul free
To learn how to look within for what I cannot see

The lives we seek are only in name
As the lives we live are all the same
With travel we find our home to blame
But it is within us that lies the shame
We refuse to leave from whence we came
And continue to play the same old game
Though we may never escape all the same
The choice of team can change the game

We search for the eyes we dare not see
In fear they will see more than we dare to be
We search the stars for similar scars to see
But hide ours away in who we pretend to be
We search beyond sorrow, tomorrow to see
But spend today wishing away choices to be
We search for comfort in the failure to attain we see
As better than a failure at all we wished to be
We search over again refusing within to see
The secret of self, defines all that will be

Welcoming sighs this winter chill
Freeze this heart and forever be-still
Awaiting warmth of trustworthy appeal
Before we dare our soul to reveal
May words in spell be cast to deal
A tattered soul in search of real

His life lay dormant in a room
consumed of regret and rage within
A room filled with the shredded pages
of written failures on how to begin
Over and over again he searches the

scars and scraps for answers to arrange
But within the mess the only sign of
answers come together as the word change
From the repeated pages of denial
came the only song he was able to sing
While all along the song he heard within
he had already written as change one thing
In a separateness we search for life
But of community we accept what is strife
What sort of fear should draw us away
From the truth we seek without price to pay
For the crowd you follow, even if in part
Will never lead to what is best for your heart
Walk alone or with kindred souls
Staying true to the path of your life goals

To see the world through a younger man's eyes
But the reflection in others you cannot deny
To hear in the world the slowing sand's cries
Yet the heart keeps urging you continue to try
And seek what soothes you in spite of the whys

The beauty of life is not of journey or acquisition
But in the silent moments in between of our personal transition
But it is only when we draw near that allusion of destination
Do we encounter the truth forever hidden in silent recollection

The wind blows through the fences of life
That we see as our defense against strife
But it doesn't protect against feelings that flow
And cause the stirring of our soul to grow
Look for fences and that is all you will ever see
Look for the gates and see your soul set free

I suppose one can find solace in always picking up the pieces
But in doing so the quest of our own dreams surely ceases
The untruths we harbor just to keep the status quo
Do nothing but build bridges to the point where nothing makes sense but letting it go
All recognition becomes a reflection of only the pieces you've collected
And any true sense of who you are becomes lost and neglected

So, if you have time to start over remember to focus on you
And if not seek you in everything new

Is there even a point to the search for life's moments
Or is life merely an accidental chain of events
Is there any reason for the search for purpose or place in the design
Or is this another untruth we believe to occupy the short time before we resign
One might imagine the better purpose for it
Would be to release the energy to one whom might better use it
But that would just carry the circle on
Without much hope of learning from energy gone

Someday perhaps we all shall learn
How to choose that which we give concern
The trivial things we take so personal
Are nothing more than all things intrapersonal
Our attention is drawn by the wants of a few
Instead of the needs our heart holds true
So, when we learn to follow our heart
.No longer shall we be a world apart

Steadily the ship, downhill shall sail
Despite the uphill fight tooth and nail
Consumed we become of tasked to bail
The helm alone must steer from storms that wail
The winds whispers grow strong of fail
Urging choice of steer to bail or drown to mainsail
Both born and die from such travailing

In the wake of new beginnings
Stir the ghosts of past misgivings
Moments of noise they wait and hide
In silence release a drowning tide
Resistance tells the same tale of grim
Silent hope is risking the swim

Every day we get closer to choosing
Loosening grip on thoughts of losing
We think we must have a plan
But freedom is the absence of sand
To those who ask what will you do
Our reply shall be whatever we choose to

It takes 20 miles of every run
To let go of what life has done
But then begins with every mile
The bonding with my inner smile
My dream on day is to ride forever
But until the day I say now or never

Difficult it is to find your place
Among things defining or space
Some things are lost without a trace
Others never existed for our embrace
Searchers aspire to a prejudice pace
Those who befriend the mirrored face
Learn that within we are the place
And ourselves we don't need to chase

Lost is he who seeks differently from the rest
As in an ear to share thoughts on life's quest
Age and appearance are not what sets us free
But a soul into which one can truly see
Some seek only what they might see
While another inspires all that we might be
It's not about the duration of time
But merely the moments of time

It's not what you own or possess
But the secrets and truths you confess
Lost is not to seek the touch of a passer by
But the embrace of one standing by
Lost is a place where only few have time
And patience to wait till the words do rhyme

The edge to find some encourage you
The edge live on we think I
Almost say we those words
Almost take we those risks
Hold on do we things safe to perceive
Hold on would we to let go better off things

In those moments anticipating the thunder
A light provokes the heart and soul a sunder
The heart clings to hope and passion perceived
But in life, sight and sound never fall the same
Leaving the learning lesson of not holding the future to blame
It will never be about asking for what we receive
It will always be about choosing in what we believe
It will never be about questioning of what we perceive
It will always be about aspiring to what we conceive

It will never be about arriving to what we may reprieve
It will always be about journeying in what we retrieve
It will never be about settling for what we grieve
It will always be about accepting what chooses to deceive
It is about seeing in today's lessons our path to it will

Chaos lingers as the repetitive rhyme
Logic abandons all hope for a reason
Wasting become the perception of time
Darkness and shadow are the season
Past grows regretfully large upon the climb
Tears of the soul cried softly of the treason

From a blankness where the requirements of the day reside
Lives beyond the resistance those moments we can set them aside
And relish in the silence where our truths and secrets may hide
And become lost in the vastness of whom we may see on the inside
As we feel the colors of our soul explode beyond any rules to abide

And it is here we find the courage and strength to again
face the outside

With kindness she searched my soul and ask me to smile
I responded in kind and asked if I could borrow hers for a
while
It felt pretty good until I began seeing the shadows of
denial
In her shadows I realized from the walk in her shoes for a
mile
Things don't have to be perfect or bright to share your own
smile

Eagerly, it seems, are we for someone to tell our story
As if with the possibility of understanding do we find glory
Awaiting the release or vindication found in a judge's
decision
As we tell the story of how we came with calculated
precision
To be felt sorry for will never satisfy the need for desired
attraction
That comes from the light of who you are today without
distraction

Character evolves from the passion and enthusiasm for today we share
And not the vacation descriptions of life we traveled in getting there
The judge and jury you seek will always be a reflection away within you
So, let go of the rehearsal and wing it in the image of the best of you

I had learned to hide the good things I feel
Away from things or those eager to steal
As thieves care not about what I may conceal
But what I outwardly share holds the appeal
But then I was surrounded by stolen things unreal
In a darkness where my soul would congeal
So, I decided to escape the hidden and my soul reveal
And share how I feel with all who would steal
And change my world to one of unique appeal
No longer alone but surrounded by souls ethereal

In the moments of empty space does my soul give relentless chase
Like a disciplined addiction seeking nothing more than my attention
Hoping I may hear the thought that changes the direction I should steer
As the journey of the moon on its path of keeping the earth in tune
But like the moon we embark understanding that some things remain dark
And we choose from our soul's insight what best serves us in the light

Could you learn to trust another with your wants and needs
Could you believe in another enough to share your dreams
Could you learn that mistakes offer growth as flowers from seeds
Could you release a love that solely in another's eyes beams
All and nothing to offer but a heart of truth and warmth it bleeds
And a soul locked away awaiting the key to more than it seems
A reflection in darkness unseen until a touch of light it feeds
And evolves in the spirt of colorful sunsets and gleaming moonbeams

It is when we release from a life pressed up against the glass
That we begin to understand the pain and suffering we amass
The aches of desire and expectation ease upon release of the fight
Visions bleed and tingle along paths long blocked from sight
Hypnotized we are caught up in the grasp of a storied show
And limit the scope of life that does internally and uniquely flow
Step away and look beyond the outline of your smudged reflection
Follow the path offering no resistance to your life's true distinction

In the beginning he knew what he thought it meant
To always be busy through every moment spent
But to be wrong did not really feel that brand new
But more like an experience not unlike that of Déjà vu
Silent moments were short lived in busy days of long
But the longer the moments the louder the silent song
In verses of regret, betrayal, and enough to never be
Hidden away in the silence of too busy to ever see

A diamond waiting for the dirt to unfold
And reveal a soul of beauty untold
Some come close as every breath held dear
And wait until silence is all there is to hear
Life be cursed for all the time and work to be unfound

But life responds silently in the pronounced heartbeat sound
As it follows not the rules that come from goal
But awaits the day from silence comes the soul

The stranger alone on a familiar road
Watching the edge of darkness erode
The lights of a city still faint in the distance
But the sounds of life fall beyond existence
In the moments of peace before the celebration
He reflects in pause before his pending obligation
And gives thanks in the light of each rising sun
Not just in the one popular opinion does run
And casts his dreams into the light of every moon
As a lone wolf howls his ancient rune

We search of youth for meanings in connection
But turn away from the light of age as our reflection
Of limiting beliefs, we cast ourselves unto rejection
And create our own life of timid subjection

Another day of pointless bound
Oblivious to any soulful sound
Fleeting is passion where no growth is found
Yet we remain silent amidst the crowned
Settling for words occasionally profound
Until we escape the merry-go-round
Heavy of heart, by soul turned cold
Are many a story of life left untold
Of choices made poorly to unfold
Open and honest with horns of gold
Future portrayed of loyalty surely sold
Or uninspired with halo broken and cold
But in need of a future to forever hold
No one is perfect in any story to be told
Broken halos are horns waiting to unfold

Love for me stopped long ago
Legally my name would you no longer go
Your stolen life I must surely owe
As we differ completely on things to show
My soul from coal did this journey bestow
And forgotten of you anything to let go